Schritte 2
international

Glossary XXL
Deutsch–Englisch
German–English

Hueber Verlag

English Translation and Adaption:
Jeannie Sanke

Authors:
Sophie Caesar (Familiarity and Understanding, Getting It All Down)
María Jesús Gil Valdés (Listening and Pronunciation)
Christiane Seuthe (Forms and Structures)
Wilfried Völker (Historical Fragments)

Quellen:
Seite 10:   Fotos: links: Marion Kerner, München; rechts: Sylvette Penning-Hiemstra, Bremen
Seite 18:   Foto: © René Lamb
Seite 28:   Foto: © irisblende.de
Seite 29:   Foto oben: © irisblende.de; Foto unten: © MEV/MHV
Seite 30:   Foto oben: © Konrad Adenauer-Stiftung/ACDP; unten © picture-alliance/akg-images
Seite 31:   Foto links: © picture-alliance/dpa; rechts: © Konrad Adenauer-Stiftung/ACDP
Seite 51:   Fotos: oben: © MEV/MHV; mitte: © irisblende.de; unten: © Wuppertaler Stadtwerke AG
Seite 60:   Fotos: oben: © Kurverwaltung Mölln, Hindenburgstraße, 23879 Mölln; unten: © Interfoto/Rauch
Seite 61:   Fotos: oben: © Interfoto/Foto; unten: © picture-alliance/akg-images
Seite 71:   Foto: © Interfoto/Archiv Friedrich
Seite 80:   © irisblende.de
Alle anderen Fotos: Alexander Keller, München

4. 3. 2. | Die letzten Ziffern
2013 12 11 10 09 | bezeichnen Zahl und Jahr des Druckes.
Alle Drucke dieser Auflage können, da unverändert,
nebeneinander benutzt werden.
1. Auflage
© 2009 Hueber Verlag, 85737 Ismaning, Deutschland
Zeichnungen: Jörg Saupe, Düsseldorf
Layout: Erwin Schmid, Hueber Verlag, Ismaning
Satz: Typosatz W. Namisla GmbH, München
Redaktion: CoLibris-Lektorat Dr. Barbara Welzel, Göttingen
Druck und Bindung: Ludwig Auer GmbH, Donauwörth
Printed in Germany
ISBN 978-3-19-451852-0

Preface

Dear Learner,

in this **XXL Glossary** you will find, as its title suggests, much more than just a glossary. Each chapter includes the following sections:

Vocabulary

All new words are presented in the order in which they appear in both the course book and the workbook, page-by-page, then alphabetically. Unlike a dictionary, this glossary allows you to learn words in context so that their meaning is far more real to you than a dictionary entry.

Forms and Structures

In this section, we explain grammar based on concrete examples from the course book and compare and contrast the structures with those of English. As the course proceeds, you will find continued reference in newer sections to material in previous chapters to help reinforce your understanding and mastery of these points.

We have also included additional translation **exercises** in each chapter to help you get a better sense of your progress and mastery, allowing you to see more how German and English are similar and different.

Listening and Speaking

As important as grammar, structure, and vocabulary are, without knowing the sound system, they are of no use. In this section, we aim to give you the tools you will need not only to recognize the sounds of German, but to reproduce them so that you can be understood, even when your structural knowledge is weak.

Getting It All Down

In this section, we provide numerous suggestions for helping you to learn German more effectively. As the program progresses, you will find some methods that work for you, perhaps some that do not, but you will add to your arsenal of study strategies. We place particular emphasis on the use of a *Lerntagebuch* (study journal) throughout.

Familiarity and Understanding

No language exists apart from the culture in which it is couched. Here you will learn about the German-speaking areas of the world, their literature and arts, and aspects of daily life. This section also aspires to help you avoid common missteps that many foreigners and learners make.

Self-Evaluation

At the end of each chapter, you have the opportunity to evaluate your progress on the objectives in each unit, allowing you to give extra attention to and/or seek extra help in areas where you are not as confident in your new skills.

We hope that you find this volume helps you learn German with greater ease and more enjoyment, and we wish you every success.

Sincerely,

the authors and editors

Contents

Contents

Kursbuch	Textbook
Seite 7	**page 7**
die Ausbildung, -en	education
das Fernsehen (nur Singular)	*television*
die Maskenbildnerin, -nen	*make-up artist (female)*
die Nennung, -en	mention (something being named)
der Papagei, -en	*parrot*
der Schreiner, -	*carpenter*
seit	since
die Tierärztin, -nen	*veterinarian (female)*
Seite 8	**page 8**
der Kollege, -n	colleague
der Superjob, -s	*super job*
Seite 9	**page 9**
bekommen; er hat bekommen	to receive
die Blume, -n	flower
der Blumenladen, -̈en	*flower shop*
das Filmstudio, -s	*movie studio*
der Job, -s	job (usually more part-time)
der Kurier, -e	*courier, delivery person*
liefern	to deliver
die Realität, -en	*reality*
wenig	little (quantity)
wütend	furious
Seite 10	**page 10**
angestellt	employed
arbeitslos	unemployed
der Architekt, -en	*architect*
der Arzt, -̈e	physician, medical doctor (male)
die Ärztin, -nen	physician, medical doctor (female)
der Exportkaufmann, -leute	*executive in the field of exporting*
die Flugbegleiterin, -nen	*flight attendant*
die Hausfrau, -en	housewife, homemaker
der Hotelfachmann, -leute	*trained and educated hotel employee*
das Interview, -s	interview
der Journalist, -en	journalist
die Kauffrau, -en	*businesswoman*
der Kaufmann, -leute	*businessman*
noch nicht	not yet
die Programmiererin, -nen	*programmer (female)*
selbstständig	independent, self-employed
die Stelle, -n	position
unterrichten	to instruct, teach
die Verkäuferin, -nen	saleswoman, sales clerk
von Beruf	by profession/training
zur Schule gehen; er ist zur Schule gegangen	to go to school

Seite 11	page 11
die Bewerbung, -en	application
der Dativ, -e	*dative case*
das Diplom, -e	*diploma (in Europe, similar to a master's degree)*
gerade	just, currently
heiraten	to marry
das Kursalbum, -alben	*class album*
das Marketing (nur Singular)	*marketing*
die Marketing-Abteilung, -en	*marketing department*
mit freundlichen Grüßen	Sincerely/Very truly yours
der Personalchef, -s	*Director of Human Resources*
die Polin, -nen	*Pole (female)*
der Praktikant, -en	intern (male)
die Praktikantin, -nen	intern (female)
Sehr geehrter Herr ...	Dear Mr. ...
seit wann?	since when?
die Verfügung, -en	*availability, disposal*
wann?	when?
wie lange?	how long?
die Wirtschaft (nur Singular)	*here:* economics
zur Verfügung stehen; er hat zur Verfügung gestanden	*to be at one's disposal, available*
Seite 12	**page 12**
der Arbeiter, -	worker
baden	to bathe
bereit sein; er ist bereit gewesen	to be ready
der Berg, -e	mountain
Bulgarien (nur Singular)	*Bulgaria*
die Feier, -n	celebration, party
das Fest, -e	fest, party
glücklich	happy
die Hochzeit, -en	wedding
die Lebensgeschichte, -n	*life story*
die Leidenschaft, -en	*passion*
mit·schreiben; er hat mitgeschrieben	*to write along (with someone else)*
der Partyservice, -s	*party service*
das Präteritum, Präterita	*imperfect past tense, preterit tense*
der See, -n	lake
der Stift, -e	*here:* writing implement
verkaufen	to sell
Seite 13	**page 13**
der Anfang, -̈e	beginning
der April (nur Singular)	April
der August (nur Singular)	August
das Au-pair-Mädchen, -	*au pair*
das Auslandspraktikum, -praktika	*internship or practicum in a foreign country*
das Automobil, -e	*automobile*
betragen; du beträgst, er beträgt, er hat betragen	to amount to
sich bewerben, du bewirbst dich, er bewirbt sich, er hat sich beworben	to apply for

die Bildung (nur Singular)	education
die Branche, -n	industry, economic sector
die Computerkenntnisse (nur Plural)	computer skills (i.e., using software)
der Dezember (nur Singular)	December
die Dienstleistung, -en	supply of services
enden	to end
erforderlich	necessary, required
der Februar (nur Singular)	February
der Führerschein, -e	drivers license
die Germanistik (nur Singular)	Germanic Studies
die Informatik (nur Singular)	Information Studies (Computer Science)
die Informatikkenntnisse (nur Plural)	computer skills (i.e., programming)
der Januar (nur Singular)	January
der Juli (nur Singular)	July
der Juni (nur Singular)	June
der Kindergarten, ¨en	kindergarten
die Mitte, -n	middle
der November (nur Singular)	November
online	online
die Pädagogik, -en	pedagogy
die Praktikumsdauer (nur Singular)	length of the practicum/internship
der Schwerpunkt, -e	emphasis
das Semester, -	semester
der September (nur Singular)	September
der Sommermonat, -e	summer month
die Spanischkenntnisse (nur Plural)	language ability in Spanish
die Sportagentur, -en	sports agency
das Sportbusiness (nur Singular)	the sports business
das Sportevent, -s	sporting event
sportlich	sporty, athletic
die Sportreise, -n	sports trip, sports-related travel
die Vereinbarung, -en	agreement
die Verkaufsaktion, -en	sales initiative/push
die Wirtschaftskenntnisse (nur Plural)	knowledge of economics

Seite 14 — page 14

der Computerfan, -s	computer fan
dauern	to last
draußen	outside
der Fahrradhelm, -e	cycling helmet
der Fahrradkurier, -e	bike courier
die Freude, -n	joy; here: enjoyment, pleasure
führen	to lead
füttern	to feed
der Game-Designer, -	game designer
die Grafik, -en	graphics
kaufmännisch	commercial
die Kenntnis, -se	knowledge, skills
die Kreativität (nur Singular)	creativity
der Kunde, -n	customer
die Musikhochschule, -n	institute for the study of music

die Ortskenntnis, -se	knowledge of the area
das Paket, -e	package
pflegen	to care for
die Puppe, -n	puppet, doll
der Puppenspieler, -	puppeteer (male)
die Puppenspielerin, -nen	puppeteer (female)
die Regenkleidung (nur Singular)	rain clothes, rain gear
das Schaf, -e	sheep
der Schäfer, -	shepherd
die Schafwolle, -n	sheep's wool
die Schnelligkeit (nur Singular)	speed
die Sicherheit, -en	safety, security
der Spezialrucksack, ¨e	special backpack
der Straßenverkehr (nur Singular)	street traffic
das Stück, -e	piece
technisch	technical
das Tier, -e	animal
der Traum, ¨e	dream
überhaupt	here: at all
ungewöhnlich	unusual
das Wissen (nur Singular)	knowledge
die Wolle (nur Singular)	wool

Seite 15 — page 15

modal: die modale Präposition	modal: modal preposition
die Nachsilbe, -n	suffix
das Private (nur Singular)	private, personal things
temporal: die temporale Präposition	temporal: temporal preposition
die Wortbildung, -en	word construction

Seite 16 — page 16

der Automechaniker, -	auto mechanic
backen; er hat gebacken	to bake
der Bäcker, -	baker
einzeln	individual (adj.)
der Elektriker, -	electrician
der Fleischer, -	butcher
der Fleischhauer, -	butcher (Austrian)
das Frühstücksbrötchen, -	breakfast roll
das Haar, -e	hair
der Metzger, -	butcher
das Motorrad, ¨er	motorcycle
müssen; du musst, er muss	must
reparieren	to repair
die Steckdose, -n	electrical outlet
der Strom (nur Singular)	electricity

Seite 17 — page 17

der Bauarbeiter, -	construction worker
davon	here: of them
die Einzelfigur, -en	individual figure
die Eisenindustrie (nur Singular)	iron industry
die Fabrik, -en	factory
die Figur, -en	figure, figurine

die Figurengruppe, -n	*group of figures or figurines*
der Hausbau (nur Singular)	*home construction*
ihn	him
der Lösungsbuchstabe, -n	*letter in the answer*
der Maurer, -	*mason*
norddeutsch	North German
der Schmied, -e	*smith*
der Schuhmacher, -	*shoemaker*
der Schuster, -	*shoemaker, cobbler*
die Stahlindustrie (nur Singular)	*steel industry*
die Szene, -n	scene
tausendjährig	*thousand-year-old*
das Thema, Themen	theme, topic
vor·stellen	to introduce
westlich	*west*
die Zinnfigur, -en	*tin figurine*
das Zinnfigurenmuseum, -museen	*museum of tin figurines*
die Zinnfigurensammlung, -en	*collection of tin figurines*

Arbeitsbuch

Workbook

Seite 84

page 84

mexikanisch	*Mexican*

Seite 86

page 86

die Katze, -n	cat
das Schulfest, -e	*school festival*

Seite 87

page 87

der Sprachkurs, -e	*language course*

Seite 88

page 88

der Geburtstagskalender, -	*birthday calendar*

Seite 89

page 89

die Arbeitszeit, -en	*work time*
das Call Center, -	*call center*
der Telefonist, -en	*telephone receptionist*
die Textstelle, -n	*text passage*
der Traumjob, -s	*dream job*

1   Nouns: formation *(Nomen: Wortbildung)*

examples

der Freund	–	*die Freundin*	plural:	*die Freundinnen*
der Journalist	–	*die Journalistin*		*die Journalistinnen*
der Arzt	–	*die Ärztin*		*die Ärztinnen*
der Spanier	–	*die Amerikanerin*		*die Amerikanerinnen*

In Chapters 3 and 4, we saw that a noun's gender is not indicated by the physical gender of the object named, and very rarely can be determined by anything in the noun itself. In the case of nouns referring to people, there are masculine and feminine forms of nouns describing profession, ethnicity, relationship, and other categories. The feminine form is formed by adding the suffix *-in* to the masculine noun. In some cases, an umlaut will also be added to the stem *(Ärztin)*. To form their plurals, these feminine forms will double the final *-n-* before adding the *-en (Freundinnen)*.

examples

der Kaufmann	–	*die Kauffrau*	
der Hausmann	–	*die Hausfrau*	

Other nouns of profession whose masculine form is a compound with *Mann,* such as *Kaufmann,* will replace the *-mann* with *-frau* to form the feminine equivalent.

2   The *Präteritum* of the verbs *sein* and *haben*

use

examples

Das hast du gut gemacht.	You did that well.
*Du **warst** prima!*	You were great!
*Der Urlaub **war** toll. Wir **hatten** 30 Grad und haben jeden Tag gebadet.*	Vacation was great. It was 30 degrees and we went swimming every day.

In Chapter 7, we learned the past tense, *das Perfekt*. This tense is used overwhelmingly in spoken communication (and in informal written texts such as personal letters, postcards or e-mails) for talking about events in the past.
In contrast, the verbs *sein* and *haben* usually use the *Präteritum* in the past tense instead of the *Perfekt*.

It is important to note here that just because the *Perfekt* is a compound construction, this does not impact the translation or usage. In the examples above, you can see that *hast ... gemacht* still translates in English as "did". Compound English tenses (have done, was doing, used to do) do **not** correspond to compound German tenses. Remember: it is essential to translate *meaning*, not individual words.

forms

The *Präteritum* of the verb *sein* is built upon the stem *war* (from the same root as our form *was*), and then takes the same endings as the modal verbs (like *können*) do in the present tense.

ich	*war*	–	compare:	*(kann)*
du	*warst*	*-st*		*(kannst)*
er/es/sie	*war*	–		*(kann)*
wir	*waren*	*-en*		*(können)*
ihr	*wart*	*-t*		*(könnt)*
sie/Sie	*waren*	*-en*		*(können)*

The verb *haben* uses as its *Präteritum* stem *hat-* followed by another *-t-* and the same endings we have seen in the forms of *möchte*.

ich	hatte	-t-e	compare:	(möchte)
du	hattest	-t-est		(möchtest)
er/es/sie	hatte	-t-e		(möchte)
wir	hatten	-t-en		(möchten)
ihr	hattet	-t-et		(möchtet)
sie/Sie	hatten	-t-en		(möchten)

3 The modal preposition: *als* + nominative (*Modale Präposition*)

examples   *Ich mache eine Ausbildung **als** Hotelfachfrau.*   I'm doing a training course as a hotel professional.

*Er ist Programmierer, aber er arbeitet **als** Techniker.*   He is a programmer, but he works as a technician.

The preposition *als* is used before nouns (with no article) to designate professions. It is always followed by a nominative noun. *als* appears in combination with the verb *arbeiten* or in expressions such as *eine Ausbildung machen* or *eine Stelle haben/suchen* or *einen Job haben/suchen*.

4 Temporal prepositions: *vor, seit* + dative (*Temporale Präpositionen*)

examples   ***Wann** haben Sie geheiratet?*   When did you get married?
   *– **Vor** einem Jahr.*   – A year ago.

***Wann** bist du aus dem Urlaub gekommen?*   When did you get back from vacation?
*– **Vor** drei Wochen.*   – Three weeks ago.

The preposition *vor* is used in response to the question *wann?* to refer to time elapsed since the action occured. In German, it is a preposition, meaning that it comes *before* its object. In English, we use "ago", which is a postposition, meaning it follows its object.

example   ***Wann** hast du Geburtstag?*   When is your birthday?
   *– **Im** November.*   – In November.

In response to the question *wann?* the prepositions *im, am* and *um* that we learned in Chapter 5 are used to construct various time expressions:

am Montag, am Wochenende *am Nachmittag*	*am* + days of the week + times of day (exception: *in der Nacht*)
um zehn (Uhr)	*um* + clock times
im Juli *im Sommer* *im Jahr 2000*	*im* + months + seasons + years

examples　*Wann haben Sie Ihr Diplom gemacht?*　Wenn did you earn your degree?
　　　　　– 1998.　　　　　　　　　　　　– In 1998.

　　　　　Meine Eltern haben 1984 geheiratet.　My parents (got) married in 1984.

When a year is given without the expression *im Jahr*, no preposition is used.
English is slowly beginning to influence a change in this practice.

From 1100 to 1999, years are given in the hundreds:
1100 elf/hundert,
1999 neunzehn/hundert/neunundneunzig

Years prior to 1100 or after 1999 are read as numbers would be:
1099 tausend/neunundneunzig
2001 zweitausend/eins

examples　**Seit wann** *lernen Sie Deutsch?*　*How long have you been learning German?*
　　　　　– Seit *einem Jahr.*　　　　　　　*– For a year.*

　　　　　Wie lange *kennst du Pablo schon?*　*How long have you known Pablo?*
　　　　　– Seit *zehn Jahren.*　　　　　　　*– For ten years.*

seit translates literally as "since" but is used differently in German. In response to the question *wie lange?* (how long), *seit* indicates that the occasion has thus far lasted since the time it began until the present. Remember in Chapter 2, (XXL Glossary, p. 28), the notion that having lived somewhere for a long time is a *present-tense* activity in German. This concept applies here too when there is a question of *seit wann?* or *wie lange?*

In the second example, the word *schon* is a modal particle that serves to reinforce the notion that this present-tense action has been going on for some time. It does not always translate.

examples　*Hast du eine Uhr?*　　　　　　Do you have a watch?
　　　　　Ich warte schon seit ein Uhr.　I have been waiting since one o'clock.
　　　　　*Ich warte schon seit einer **Stunde**.*　I have been waiting for an hour (already).

In German, (*die*) *Uhr* refers to the clock, much as English refers to clock time as "x o'clock [of the clock]". The passage of 60 minutes, one hour, is expressed as (*die) Stunde*. Do not be confused by the rather deceptive similarity in sound of "hour" and *Uhr*.

Almost all temporal prepositions in German take objects in the dative case.
Like the nominative and accusative cases, the dative case also has characteristic markers accompanying the noun. Plural nouns have markers as well.

vor, seit + dative	m	n	f	pl	
Ich lerne seit	*einem Monat*	*einem Jahr*	*einer Woche*	*Jahren*	*Deutsch.*
Er war vor	*einem Monat*	*einem Jahr*	*einer Stunde*	*zehn Minuten*	*hier.*

When answering *wie lange?* questions without a preposition, the nouns indicating time are accusative:

examples　*Wie lange lernen Sie schon Deutsch? – **Einen** Monat./Ein Jahr.*
　　　　　Wie lange kennst du Pablo schon? – Zehn Jahre.

5   The temporal preposition *für* + accusative

examples   *Ich suche **für** einen Monat ein Praktikum.*   I'm looking for an internship for one month.
(I'm looking for a one-month internship.)

Ich suche eine Ferienwohnung.   I'm looking for a vacation apartment.
*– **Für wie lange**?*   – For how long?
Für vierzehn Tage.   For fourteen days.

When talking about an anticipated duration of time (as opposed to a duration that started in the past and is continuing now), Germans use *für*. It does not correspond to all our temporal uses of "for", so watch its usage carefully. It is also one of the few temporal prepositions in German which takes accusative objects. It is used in response to the question *für wie lange?*

To give a beginning and an ending time of a duration, the prepositions *von ... bis* (from ... until/till), that we learned in Chapter 5, are appropriate.
Again, the corresponding questions are *wie lange?* or *von wann bis wann?*

examples   *Von wann bis wann waren Sie in Südamerika?*   From when till when were you in South America?
– Von 1985 bis 1989.   – From 1985 till 1989.

Wie lange habt ihr Ferien?   How long do you have vacation (for)?
– Von Juni bis September.   – From June till September.

6   Complements of the verb *sein*

examples   *Ist Frau Söll da?*   Is Ms. Söll there?
– Tut mir leid, sie ist im Moment nicht da.   – I'm sorry, at the moment she's not.

Fernando hat in Australien gelebt.   Fernando lived in Australia.
– Ach ja? Wie lange war er denn da?   – Oh, really? How long was he there?

Aside from the famous Descartes quote ("I think, therefore I am") the verb *sein*, like the English verb "be", is usually followed by a complement, something to make the sentence whole. This can be an an adverb or prepositional phrase, as in the examples above (*da, im Büro*). There can also be other nouns, known as predicate nominative in English, that are the equivalent of the subject (*Das ist mein Mann./Ich bin Studentin.*) or an adjective (*Das Wetter ist schön.*).

7   **Translate into English.**

a *Mein Bruder war im Sommer in Mexiko.* ....

Er macht eine Ausbildung als ....

Hotelfachmann und hat in Cancún ein ....

Praktikum gemacht. Er hat da wirklich ....

viel gelernt. ....

b *Sonia, du suchst doch einen Job,* ....

nicht? Die Firma Servitec braucht ....

Leute mit guten Sprachkenntnissen. ....

Ich habe eine Anzeige im Internet ....

gefunden. ....

8   **Translate into German.**

a How long are you in Germany for? ....

– For three months. ....

And what are you studying? ....?

– I'm studying economics and marketing. ....

You're doing an internship at Siemens, ...*bei Siemens*................*, nicht* ?

right? How long have you been studying? ....?

– Four weeks. ....

b What did you do on the weekend? ....?

– I had a visit. A friend from Switzerland ....

was here and we talked a lot. What did ....*haben*................*erzählt* .

you do? ....?

– We were at a wedding. It was very ....

lovely. We danced until five in the ....*schön.*....................

morning. ....*morgens*........................... .

Listening and Pronunciation

Pronunciation of final <e> and final <r>

gehe ● *Schule*

If a word with more than one syllable ends with the vowel <e>, it is very short and completely unstressed. In Chapter 6, we looked at the shwa (see pg. 67 of the XXL-Glossary, Volume 1); the same sound applies here.

er ● *wir*

When the consonant <r> appears at the end of the word, it sounds more like an <a> then a consonant. The phenomenon is the same as the so-called "Boston R".

Bruder ● *Programmierer*

The combination <er> is especially common at the ends of words. Again, the <a> sound, or the Boston R, is correct here.

Syllabic stress in compound nouns

Mann   *Fachmann*   *Hotelfachmann*
Frau   *Kauffrau*   *Exportkauffrau*

Remember: in compound nouns, even though each noun on its own had its own stress, when combined, it is usually the stress of the first noun that becomes the stressed syllable for the entire, compound word.

Getting It All Down

Seit – vor

It would be worth your while at this point to make a table of the temporal prepositions that you learned in Chapter 5 (*am*, *um*) and expand it to include the ones from this unit (*vor, seit*). Vocabulary cards with these prepositions should have contextual examples on them so that you can learn their application, and get used to dative objects with them, as you learn them.

Reading comprehension strategies

When reading a text in German, you want to concentrate on the most important information. Coding key information in color, making notes with your own words and not just those in the text and looking for repeating items are a few excellent strategies. Before you just start looking up every word you don't know, however, at least read the passage through a couple of times. Even in early stages of language learning, there is more passive knowledge at work than you realize. Use it to your advantage.

Familiarity and Understanding

Handwerk hat goldenen Boden

The skilled labor sector in Germany is made up of over 100 officially recognized, regulated, title-granting professional organizations.
In order to become a professional tradesman, one must complete an obligatory course of study, lasting usually three years, at an accredited vocational school, including passing a final examination.
Completion of vocational education qualifies candidates for employment in their respective fields. However, in order to train apprentices or manage a business, the title of *Meister* is required in most professions. Pursuing *Meister* status requires further practical experience of weeks or months to ensure a level of skill and professionalism commensurate with the higher liability inherent in the *Meister's* duties.

Students interested in learning a trade can apply to any of the 1600 *Berufsschulen* (vocational schools) in Germany. These schools combine theoretical education with parallel practical training as an apprentice, or *Azubi* (short for *Auszubildende/r*) in a factory, workshop, or other professional environment. Depending upon the particular course of study, students may work three to four days per week and spend one or two days in classroom settings.

During this course of study, students receive financial compensation from the company hosting the apprenticeship. This remuneration can vary greatly — anywhere from 150 euros per month for a photographer's apprentice to 600 euros per month for a third-year auto mechanic's apprentice (which also includes training on the electronic components of automobiles).

The five most sought-after professions among young Germans pursuing vocational education are: (1) auto mechanic, (2) hairdresser/barber, (3) electrician, (4) painter/varnisher, and (5) heating and air conditioning technician.

There are over 800,000 companies employing more than 5 million skilled tradesmen and -women. These workers comprise 15% of the total population. Many of Germany's young people opt for this type of training; positions are almost always secure and income is high. Unfortunately, in some areas of specialization, there is a shortage of apprenticeships and this in turn contributes to rising unemployment among youth.

Other non-academic options

There are numerous non-academic professions requiring 9 to 10 years of education as opposed to 12 (to take the *Abitur*). Several areas, such as service industries (banking, insurance, various commercial enterprises) and the healthcare sector offer other options for young people seeking a career. Including skilled labor professions, there are 355 non-academic professions that carry recognized titles, such as Laboratory Technician, Nurse, Insurance Broker, and even Teller (much more prestigious than in the U.S.). All these professions require vocational as well as education-based training. In all, 70% of young Germans choose to pursue specialized training outside the university or *Fachhochschule* environment.

University: Bachelor and Master

In Germany, there are ca. 370 so-called *Hochschulen*. These are not high schools, but rather institutions of higher learning beyond the secondary level, encompassing not only universities (approx. 100), but also *Fachhochschulen* (approx. 170) that offer programs leading to the degree of *Diplom* in engineering and technical fields. The *Diplom* is a degree that would be higher than an American M.S. but less than the Ph.D. There are also *Hochschulen* for various arts as well.

During the 2007/2008 academic year, approximately 2.2 million students were registered and matriculated in Germany, but that number is declining due to federal reforms and the rise in matriculation fees (approximately € 500 per semester), giving ever more potential applicants pause. The massive increase in fees (though still practically nothing by U.S. standards) has been intended to slow enrollment in overcrowded programs with the aim of improving the quality of education.

Like those in other European countries, the universities in the German-speaking countries offer Master's degrees (usually requiring 10 or more semesters of study) as well as doctoral degrees. In the last several years, the Bachelor's degree, requiring about 6 semesters of study, has been introduced, though it is not yet widely accepted in German-language areas as a valid credential for employment.

Approximately 10% of students in Germany are foreign, the majority coming from Poland, Bulgaria and China. Of those, 83% matriculate directly, while the remaining 17% come from other organized programs or student exchanges.

Germans heading abroad to study go primarily to six countries: Great Britain, the United States, France, Austria, Spain and the Netherlands.

„*Wandel durch Austausch*": Change by exchange

The DAAD (*Deutscher Akademischer Austauschdienst* – German Academic Exchange Service) is a federally funded but independently managed organization which finances academic exchanges (both student and professorial) between German educational institutions and others abroad. It is similar in structure and mission to the Fulbright Program in the U.S. and works to encourage cross-cultural awareness and interchange along with increased interest in German language abroad. Educational cooperation with developing nations is another point of emphasis. 50,000 individuals are supported each year for studies outside of Germany or for non-Germans to study at German institutions, and some 400 DAAD instructors give classes in German language and culture at universities throughout the world.

It's very practical

Whether in an academic or vocational setting, practical experience is highly valued. Many students in Germany seek out *Praktika* either during their studies or immediately after completing their degree in order to better their chances of finding a position. Such internships of a few weeks' or months' duration are usually unpaid, but the opportunity to gain familiarity with a company, organization or particular type of work is considered to be quite valuable. Being noticed by a potential employer is even more prized. Unions tend to oppose such internships, fearing exploitation of cheap or even free labor, but it does provide a practical complement to an education that is typically more theoretical in nature. Individuals interested in working in Austria, Switzerland or Germany can often combine a German language course with an internship position. In addition to academies which arrange such packages for applicants, many companies post information about such opportunities on their own websites.

Historical Fragments

No tobacco or alcohol, and everybody profits: one Swiss business model

The *Tante-Emma-Laden* (mom-and-pop store) is quickly becoming extinct in Germany as larger *Supermärkte* offer larger selections at lower prices with longer opening hours.

In Switzerland, however, one man's dream created another model for big business. In 1925, Gottlieb Duttweiler began selling staples directly out of five trucks, sometimes at even 40% less than what the competition charged. His recipe for success was to sell the most needed products directly to the consumer at the best possible price. Knowing that Switzerland was rather puritanical, he boosted his company's reputation by refusing to sell tobacco and alcohol. Today, *Migros* stores now comprise the largest retail chain in Switzerland and one of the 500 largest corporations in the world.

In 1941, Gottlieb Duttweiler transformed *Migros* from an AG (a joint-stock company) to a cooperative in which any Swiss could hold membership and participate in management. In effect, *Migros* is owned by its customers. In 1944, *Migros* founded the *Klubschulen*, club schools, which today comprise the largest network for continuing education in Switzerland, especially for foreign languages.

This was only the first in a long string of social initiatives *Migros* undertook, under Duttweiler's direction, in Switzerland, and the company funds this work by committing 1% of sales to cultural activities. In pursuing his dream for a socially committed business model, Gottlieb Duttweiler rather single-handedly helped to create the image of Switzerland as a socially engaged and humanitarian country.

Self-Evaluation

When listening, I can understand (Hören)

– the most important points of information in a job interview

– information regarding the most significant activities in various professions

– questions about my education: *Wann haben Sie das Diplom gemacht? Wie lange arbeiten Sie schon bei „Föbis"? Seit wann machen Sie ein Praktikum?*

– specific indications of time: *Die Praxis ist von Montag bis Donnerstag geöffnet.*

In written texts, I can understand (Lesen)

– employment postings in newspapers or on the internet: *Wir suchen Praktikanten mit guten Wirtschaftskenntnissen …*

– an "employment sought" ad

– texts describing professions by way of activities and qualifications

I can produce the following oral structures (Sprechen)

– identifying my profession and asking others about theirs: *Ich bin Lehrerin von Beruf. / Ich arbeite als Verkäuferin. / Was sind Sie von Beruf?*

– describing my academic and professional education: *Ich habe Informatik studiert. / Ich mache eine Ausbildung als Hotelfachfrau.*

– statements of various times from the past: *Das war vor 15 Jahren. / Ich habe im Januar geheiratet. / Im Sommer war ich bei meinen Eltern auf dem Land.*

I can produce the following written texts (Schreiben)

– a request for more information regarding a position: *Sehr geehrte Damen und Herren, ich habe Ihre Anzeige …*

– questions for a hiring interview: *Seit wann arbeiten Sie? / Als was haben Sie gearbeitet? / Von wann bis wann haben Sie Urlaub im Jahr?*

Kursbuch	Textbook
Seite 18	**page 18**
fremd	foreign, strange
die Gemütlichkeit (nur Singular)	*hospitality, welcoming atmosphere*
das Oktoberfest, -e	*October Fest*
der Titel, -	*title*
der Tourist, -en	tourist
unterwegs	on the way from one place to another
das Volksfest, -e	*folk festival*

Seite 19	**page 19**
bayerisch	*Bavarian*
dürfen; du darfst, er darf	to be allowed; may
echt	*authentic, genuine*
original	original

Seite 20	**page 20**
die Abendkasse, -n	*evening cashier's desk*
die Architektur, -en	*architecture*
die Arena, -nen	*arena*
der Ausflug, ¨e	excursion
aus·wählen	*to select*
direkt	directly
der Dom, -e	cathedral
der Fahrkartenautomat, -en	*automated ticket vending machine*
die Führung, -en	tour
generell	*generally*
der Haushalt, -e	housekeeping
das Märchenschloss, ¨er	*fairy-tale castle*
das Rathaus, ¨er	city hall
der Ratschlag, ¨e	suggestion, piece of advice
reservieren	to reserve
speziell	*here: specifically*
die Stadtführung, -en	tour of the city
stempeln	*to stamp*
der Taxifahrer, -	*taxi driver*
die Theaterkarte, -n	*theater ticket*
unbedingt	absolutely, unconditionally
wählen	to choose
warten	to wait
das Wechselgeld (nur Singular)	*change (returned from a transaction)*
das Ziel, -e	goal, destination
zum Schluss	in conclusion, at the end

Seite 21	**page 21**
aus·machen	to turn off
das Fenster, -	window
der Gameboy, -s	*Gameboy*
der Imperativ, -e	*imperative, command form*
die Kasse, -n	cashier, register

laut	loud
leise	quiet
das Mistwetter (nur Singular)	*lousy weather*
nach·sehen; du siehst nach, er sieht nach, er hat nachgesehen	to look (in search of something)
och	aw
der Pass, ¨e	passport
der Stadtplan, ¨e	city map
das Ticket, -s	ticket (for travel)
unternehmen; du unternimmst, er unternimmt, er hat unternommen	to undertake, to do
unterschreiben; er hat unterschrieben	to sign
zu·hören	to listen
zu·machen	to close
zusammen·bleiben; er ist zusammengeblieben	to stay together

Seite 22	**page 22**
erlaubt	allowed
fotografieren	to photograph
mit·kommen; er ist mitgekommen	to come along
parken	to park
rauchen	to smoke
die Regel, -n	rule
telefonieren	to call on the phone, to use the phone
verboten	forbidden
die Zigarette, -n	cigarette

Seite 23	**page 23**
die Anreise (nur Singular)	*arrival (at the journey's end)*
besichtigen	to view
der Blick, -e	view
die Dauer (nur Singular)	length of time
die Domführung, -en	*tour of the cathedral*
der Eintritt, -e	entry
die Eintrittskarte, -n	entry ticket
der Eintrittspreis, -e	price of entry
ermäßigt	*discounted*
die Ermäßigung, -en	discount
der Feiertag, -e	holiday (day when offices are usually closed)
ganzjährig	*all year long*
die Gebühr, -en	fee
der Gottesdienst, -e	*Christian religious service*
hoch	high
die Höhe	height
die Hotline, -s	*hotline*
die Informationsbroschüre, -n	*informational brochure*
innerhalb	within
das Kammerorchester, -	*chamber orchestra*
die Kartenkategorie, -n	*ticket category*
die Kategorie, -n	*category*
das Konzert, -e	concert
der Konzertbeginn (nur Singular)	*beginning of the concert*

die Konzertkarte, -n	concert ticket
der Meter, -	meter
der Musiker, -	*musician*
ohne	without
phantastisch	*fantastic*
das Programm, -e	program
die Reisegruppe, -n	*travel group, tour group*
die Religion, -en	religion
rund	*here:* around, approximately
der Samstagabend, -e	Saturday evening
die Schulgruppe, -n	*school group*
die Sehenswürdigkeit, -en	point of interest, tourist attraction
die Sicht (nur Singular)	*view*
die Sitzplatzwahl (nur Singular)	*selection of seats*
eine Frage/Fragen stellen	*here:* pose, ask a question
südlich	*southern*
der Südturm, ⁞e	*south tower*
die Treppe, -n	staircase
der Turm, ⁞e	tower
die Turmbesteigung, -en	*tower ascent (climbing)*
während	during
das Werk, -e	(artistic) work
worüber	what about

Seite 24 — page 24

ab·geben	to turn in, submit
der Ausweis, -e	identification
das Dokument, -e	*document*
das Doppelzimmer, -	double room
das Einzelzimmer, -	single room
gehen: das geht	*here:* that'll work
das Gepäck (nur Singular)	luggage
die Halbpension (nur Singular)	half-board (room plus two meals/day)
die Hotelrezeption, -en	hotel reception desk
ideal	*ideal*
in Ordnung	in order
die Jugendherberge, -n	youth hostel
das Mehrbettzimmer, -	*room with multiple beds, shared room*
die Papiere (nur Plural)	papers
die Rezeption, -en	reception
die Schulklasse, -n	*school class (the group of students)*
die Übernachtung, -en	overnight stay
die Vollpension (nur Singular)	full-board (room plus three meals/day)

Seite 25 — page 25

gliedern	*to structure, organize*
das Pronomen, -	*pronoun*
die Zeitangabe, -n	*indication of time*

Seite 26 — page 26

die Alpen (nur Plural)	*the Alps*
das Bundesland, ⁞er	Federal state
europäisch	European
der Fasching (nur Singular)	*Shrovetide (regional)*
die Fasnacht (nur Singular)	*Shrovetide (regional)*
der Fluss, ⁞e	*river*
intensiv	*intensive*
der Karneval (nur Singular)	*Carnival (season leading up to Lent)*
das Karnevalsfest, -e	*Carnival celebration*
die Kleider (nur Plural)	clothing
die Lebensfreude, -n	*zest for life, joie de vivre*
die Nordsee (nur Singular)	*North Sea*
rheinisch	*Rhenish (relating to the Rhein region)*
der Sprachraum, ⁞e	*area where the language is spoken*
der Südwesten (nur Singular)	*Southwest*
der Teil, -e	part
wachsen; du wächst, er wächst, er ist gewachsen	to grow
der Weg, -e	way, road

Seite 27 — page 27

der Einwohner, -	inhabitant
der Kanton, -e	*canton*
die Landeshauptstadt, ⁞e	*state capital*
die Radiosendung, -en	radio broadcast
die Sendung, -en	broadcast

Arbeitsbuch — Workbook

Seite 92 — page 92

der Test, -s	test

Seite 93 — page 93

ach so	ah so/I see

Seite 94 — page 94

das Hotelzimmer, -	hotel room

Seite 96 — page 96

passend	fitting, appropriate

Seite 97 — page 97

definitiv	*definitely*
mit·fahren; du fährst mit, er fährt mit, er ist mitgefahren	to ride or travel along

Seite 98	**page 98**
der Fernsehturm, ⸚e	*TV transmission tower*

Seite 99	**page 99**
die Abreise (nur Singular)	*departure*
Irland (nur Singular)	*Ireland*
der Staat, -en	state
die Staatsangehörigkeit, -en	citizenship
voraussichtlich	*anticipated*
der Zielbahnhof, ⸚e	*train station of destination*

1 The modal verbs *müssen* and *dürfen (Modalverben)*

müssen

examples | *Meine Mutter macht den Haushalt,* | My mother keeps house
*aber ich **muss** mein Zimmer aufräumen.* | but I have to clean up my room.

*Ich **muss** noch Geld holen.* | I still have to get money.

The modal verb *müssen* corresponds to the English "must" but is more often translated as "have to", which has nothing to do with having.
In general, *müssen* is used to express an obligation (example 1) or a necessity (example 2).

examples | *Herr Ahonen, Sie **müssen unbedingt** einen* | Mr. Ahonen, you absolutely must take a trip
Ausflug nach Neuschwanstein machen. | out to Neuschwanstein.

*Wir **müssen mal** in den Dom gehen.* | We really do have to go to the cathedral.

Müssen can also be used to strongly suggest or recommend something. In this function it is combined with the adverb *unbedingt* (giving it a certain sense of importance or urgency) or the particle *mal* (making it more of a suggestion).

examples | ***Man muss** die Stadt gut kennen.* | One really has to know the city well.
| | (You really need to know the city well.)
***Man muss** die Fahrkarte hier stempeln.* | One must stamp the ticket here.
| | (You have to stamp the ticket here.)

When *müssen* appears before the impersonal pronoun *man*, it expresses a regulation or a general procedure or expectation. In English, this is usually expressed using "you have to" or "they have to" as impersonal constructions.

dürfen

examples | ***Darf** ich Sie etwas fragen?* | May I ask you something?
*Hier **dürfen** Sie rauchen.* | You're allowed to smoke here.
*Ihr **dürft** heute **nicht** fernsehen.* | You all can't watch TV today. (It's not allowed.)
*Sie **dürfen** hier **keine** Fotos machen.* | You're not allowed to take pictures here.

In Chapter 7 we saw how, when asking permission, the verb *können* can be used *(Kann ich etwas fragen?)*. In German, there is another modal, *dürfen*, which is used solely to express permission. In English, its equivalent is "may", and even though "may" is optional in English, *dürfen* in German is not, particularly when something is **not** allowed.
When *dürfen* is combined with *nicht* or *kein-*, it expresses prohibition.
When requesting permission, the use of *dürfen* is more courteous and respectful than *können* (just like in English).

As with the modal verbs you have already learned, *müssen* and *dürfen* share the same pattern of a vowel change in the singular and no ending on the 1st and 3rd person singular forms.

infinitive	*müssen*	*dürfen*	*können*	*wollen*	
ich	*muss*	*darf*	*kann*	*will*	-
du	*musst*	*darfst*	*kannst*	*willst*	*-st*
er/es/sie	*muss*	*darf*	*kann*	*will*	-
wir	*müssen*	*dürfen*	*können*	*wollen*	*-en*
ihr	*müsst*	*dürft*	*könnt*	*wollt*	*-t*
sie/Sie	*müssen*	*dürfen*	*können*	*wollen*	*-en*

2 Modal verbs in a sentence *(Modalverben im Satz)*

examples *Ich **muss** (noch) die Rechnung **bezahlen**.* I (still) have to pay the bill.
*Hier **darfst** du nur 100 **fahren**.* You're only allowed to drive 100 here.

Claudia muss morgen nach Texas (fahren). Claudia has to go to Texas tomorrow.
Darf ich zu Michaela (gehen)? May I go to Michaela?

Like all other modal verbs, *müssen* and *dürfen* are accompanied by a dependent infinitive which is always in final position.

In many cases in German, the infinitive may be omitted as it is understood, much like in English it is common to say "I have to", knowing that whatever it is that must be done is understood from the preceding part of the conversation. In German, the verbs *fahren* and *gehen* are omitted very often, even with no prior mention of the activity. In such cases, there are other complements that make the context clear (i.e., *nach Texas, zu Michaela* in the examples above).

3 The pronoun *man (Pronomen)*

examples *Als Taxifahrer muss **man** auch nachts arbeiten.* As a taxi driver, one must/you have to work nights, too.

*Im Kino muss **man** das Handy ausmachen.* In the movie theater, one has to/you have to turn off your cell phone.

*Hier kann **man** gut essen.* One can/you can eat well here.
*Hier darf **man** keine Fotos machen.* It is forbidden to/you can't take photos here.

The pronoun *man* is used to reference people or situations in general. It is a pronoun and must not be confused with the noun *(der) Mann*. The pronoun *man* functions as the subject of the sentence and the verb is conjugated in the 3rd person singular, just like for the English pronoun "one". Unlike English, using *man* in speech does not sound overly formal. Very often, we use "you" instead, or we even use passive voice or other impersonal constructions instead. The preferred usage in German is usually *man*.

4 The imperative *(Imperativ)*

examples

Gehen Sie zur Touristeninformation.
Hast du Hunger? Dann iss doch einen Apfel!
Unterschreibt bitte hier.

Go to the tourist information office.
Are you hungry? Then eat an apple!
Sign here, please.

The German imperative, or command form, functions much like the English imperative. It is important to note that there are different forms, of course, and often the German imperative will be accompanied by the words *bitte, mal* and/or *doch*. There are a few guidelines on the use of these particles but no hard and fast rules:

– Giving instructions requires no particle.
  Gehen Sie zur Touristeninformation.
  Nehmen Sie die Fahrkarte und das Wechselgeld.

– Softening a command to a suggestion can be done with *mal* and/or *doch*.
  *Machen Sie **mal** Urlaub.*
  *Gehen Sie **doch/doch mal** zur Touristeninformation.*

– For polite requests *doch, mal* and *bitte* are often used.
  *Reservieren Sie **bitte** einen Tisch.*
  *Macht **(bitte) mal** die Handys aus.*
  *Warte **doch bitte mal**.*

Generally speaking, particles soften the imperative from a blunt command or instruction.

The particle *doch* tends to highlight that, while the hearer would prefer to do something else, the speaker thinks otherwise, much like the English admonition "go on" or "go ahead, what the heck". (Attention: This stands in contrast to the *doch* that responds positively to a negative question: *Möchtest du kein Eis? – Doch.*)

In German, the imperative verb forms are identical to the present indicative forms, except for the *du*-command. Note that the *-st* ending is dropped, and if there is a stem vowel change from <e> to <i> or <ie>, it stays (but a vowel change from <a> to <ä> does not; the umlaut drops).

	imperative	present	imperative	present	imperative	present
2nd pers. sing.:	*geh!*	*(du gehst)*	*lies!*	*(du liest)*	*fahr!*	*(du fährst)*
2nd pers. plur.:	*geht*	*(ihr geht)*	*lest!*	*(ihr lest)*	*fahrt!*	*(ihr Fahrt)*
formal:	*gehen Sie!*	*(Sie gehen)*	*lesen Sie!*	*(Sie lesen)*	*fahren Sie!*	*(Sie fahren)*

For reasons of pronunciation, some verbs need an *-e* after the verb stem on the *du*-imperative. For verbs with the *-t* or *-d* on their stem, this *-e-* was already present before the *-st* ending dropped. Other verbs have simply retained a more archaic form that is more pleasing to the ear:
  warte!   *(du wartest)*
  entschuldige!   *(du entschuldigst)*

The verb *sein* forms its imperatives using the stem *sei* from the infinitive.
  sei!   *(du)*
  seid!   *(ihr)*
  seien Sie!   *(Sie)*

5   The particle *noch*

examples

Hast du die Zimmer schon reserviert?	Have you already reserved the rooms?
*– Nein, **noch** nicht.*	– No, not yet.
*Ich muss **noch** Geld holen.*	I still have to get money.
*Gibt es **noch** Karten für das Konzert?*	Are there still tickets (left) for the concert?
*Sonst **noch** etwas?*	Anything else?
– Nein danke, das ist alles.	– No, thank you, that's all.

As you can see in the examples here, there is no single equivalent in English for the German word *noch*: in the most general terms, it indicates that something is outstanding (needs to be done or has not been, items are available or that a further item is needed or in demand).
As a general rule, *noch* does not appear in first position in statements.

6   The adverb *da*

examples

Im August habe ich keine Zeit.	I don't have any time in August.
***Da** möchte ich in Urlaub fahren.*	I would like to go on vacation then.
Ich war schon mal in München.	I've already been to Munich.
***Da** gibt es das Hofbräuhaus.*	That's where the Hofbräuhaus is.
So ein Mistwetter!	What rotten weather!
***Da** kann man ja gar nichts unternehmen.*	You can't do anything in this!

The adverb *da* can have a temporal meaning (example 1), a locational significance (example 2) or a circumstantial significance (example 3).

7   Translate into English.

a   *Ihr müsst in Chicago mal das* ....

     „Hemingway House" besuchen. Da hat ....

     Ernest Hemingways Familie gewohnt. ....

b   *Frau Merten, rufen Sie doch* ....

     bitte mal bei der Information an. ....

     Vielleicht gibt es noch Karten ....

     für das Fußballspiel. ....

c   *Was bedeutet „continental breakfast"?* ....

     Bekommt man auch Orangensaft? .... ?

8   **Translate into German**

a   Excuse me, may I ask you

something? Where can you buy

admission tickets for the museum?   ....?

– I'm sorry, I don't know. It's   ....

best to ask at the tourist information   ....

office.   .... *Touristeninformation* .

b   Hey, we have to be at the   ....

restaurant at nine.   .... *im* ....

– Shoot! I forgot my purse.   ...., ... *habe* .... *vergessen* .

c   Pardon me, can you help me?   ....?

– Yes, of course.   ....

Where do you have to stamp your ticket?   ....?

Listening and Pronunciation

Sentence stress

Ich muss jetzt <u>gehen</u>.
Kannst du heute <u>kommen</u>?

In statements where there is a modal verb and an infinitive, the infinitive is the primary carrier of the information. For that reason, the sentence stress falls on the final element, the infinitive.

Intonation of imperative statements

Warten Sie einen Moment! ↘
Bitte lies den Text! ↘

As in English, imperative statements intone downward at the end.

Gehen Sie doch mal zur Touristeninformation!

Modal particles in commands are unstressed, as they are in other statements.

Getting It All Down

See you!

Some students are primarily visual learners. For such individuals, it is often very helpful to draw pictures that illustrate vocabulary or concepts, or to add the German designations to existing visual images.

Familiarity and Understanding

Gemütlichkeit

For Timo, the word *gemütlich* is tied to Munich's *Oktoberfest*, with one of its most famous songs titled *Gemütlichkeit*:

Ein Prosit, ein Prosit der Gemütlichkeit!

Though it is a German word, *Gemütlichkeit* can be found in most English dictionaries, too: it can signify friendliness, cordiality, coziness, a snug or homelike atmosphere, and so forth.
The etymology of the German expression goes back to German Romanticism and its notion of *Gemüt*. This word can refer to both the collected aspects of a human being that make it a thinking, feeling creature as well as the temperament of an individual. Thus, *gemütlich* indicates a positive view, perceived by the senses and reflected in the emotions.
For some time, the word *gemütlich* has been the standard description of German hospitality, with often subtle characteristics such as lighting candles when serving tea, creating warm, inviting rooms, and the like. G*emütlich* can also refer to an individual's temperament, when a person is calm and amiable, for example.

Germany's other national beverage

German viticulture is concentrated almost completely in the southeast and south of the country along the Rhine, Mosel and Elbe river valleys. Over 250,000 acres are devoted to growing grapes. As a comparison, vineyards cover over 939,000 acres in the United States, approximately 700,000 of which are in California. (Globally, over 17 million acres of wine grapes are grown.)

German wine-growing regions are among the northernmost in the world, and the correspondingly lower temperatures contribute to the relatively low alcohol content of German wines. 63% of German wines are white, and the most famous among those is the *Riesling*, which grows primarily high along the banks of the Rhine. The river's reflective capacity helps to maintain the high level of sunshine necessary for *Riesling* grapes. Particulary in the *Rheingau* region, situated on one of the bends in the Rhine, near Wiesbaden, conditions are optimal. *Riesling* vineyards occupy 20% of the total viticultural acreage in Germany. Its dry yet fruity taste is said to make it most suitable to be served with seafood. Germany's most famous red wine, known as *Blauer Spätburgunder,* also comes from this region.

Imported wines are also popular throughout Germany. 17% of all wine consumed is French, followed by Italian wines (16%). In third place among imports are Spanish wines at 7%.

German wines are exported around the world, with Great Britain consuming the largest share, followed by the United States and Japan.

According to some statistics, Germans consume 8 liters of German and 11 liters of imported wine per capita per year, while other reports claim 24 liters per capita per year consumption. This still places the average German far behind the French at 55 liters per capita per year.

Austria has approximately 118,000 acres of vineyards, concentrated primarily in the east of the country, around Vienna. Like Germany, white wine is grown and bottled far more than red; only one quarter of

Austria's vineyards grow red grapes. The most famous of Austria's wines is the *Grüner Veltliner*, described by some as having a peppery taste over citrus and peach.

Swiss wines are hardly known; only 2% of Swiss wine is sold outside of Switzerland. Due to the mountainous climate, it is difficult to cultivate grapes in Switzerland, and as such they grow only in the French- and Italian-speaking regions.

„Bier her!"

Anywhere in the world, when someone is asked what they associate with Germany, certainly at the top of that list stands beer. Germans consume some 120 liters of their various brews per capita each year, more than anyone else in Europe. Bavarians lead the pack with approximately 155 liters per person per year, though in fairness, Bavarian beer usually contains less alcohol than those of other regions. The strongest beer in Europe is an Austrian brew known as *Samichlaus Bier*, which has an alcohol level of 14% compared to an average of around 5%.

The oldest food law still in force throughout the world, dating from 1516, is known as the *Reinheitsgebot*. It requires maximum purity of German beer, and mandates that only four ingredients be used: water, barley, yeast and hops.

A brief glossary of beer

Some of the most popular beers in Germany are:

Weizenbier: its taste is on the sweeter side and it is primarily Bavarian, but is popular in other areas as well.

Pils: originally from Bohemia, short for *Pilsener* (from the city of Pilsen, now Plzen in the Czech Republic), one of the most popular types overall. It is also reknowned for the long wait when ordering one, as it is said that the glass must sit 7 minutes after drawing.

Kölsch: the pride of the Cologne-Bonn region, it is light in color and alcohol content (3.7%), with a slightly bitter taste.

Berliner Weiße: light in color, often mixed with raspberry juice or syrup. It is considered particularly good in warm weather.

Altbier: specific to the Düsseldorf area, it is dark and somewhat bitter.

Schwarzbier: a strong-flavored, dark-colored beer from East Germany.

Depending upon the weather, beer is frequently enjoyed outdoors in *Biergärten* during the summer. This practice is most frequently associated with Bavaria but is popular all over the country.

Historical Fragments

Two states – one new, old nation:
The Federal Republic of Germany and the German Democratic Republic (1949–1990)

Following the Allied victory over Nazi Germany in May of 1945, Europe found itself being pulled apart by superpowers on both sides; the Soviet Union dragged the East into its sphere of influence, while Western Europe allied with the United States. Between them hung what Winston Churchill first termed "the Iron Curtain," an ideological boundary which, due to the Four Powers agreement, split Germany right down the middle as well. Tensions surrounding the partition of Germany led to, among other events, the Berlin Airlift of 1948, and then to the establishment of two separate German states in 1949. The ensuing "Cold War" lasted over 40 years. The first tears in the Iron Curtain appeared with the rise of Glasnost and Perestroika within the Soviet Union, which came on the heels of the Polish Solidarity movement and then paved the way for the so-called Velvet Revolution in Hungary in 1989. The Cold War then finally ended with the reunification of the two German states on October 3, 1990.

The Basic Law of the Federal Republic (*das Grundgesetz*), which allowed for the establishment of the Federal Republic of Germany in 1949, was conceived not only as a constitution for a new German state, but also as a provisional measure until Germany could be unified as a single country again. During the tenure of the first Chancellor of the Federal Republic of Germany, **Konrad Adenauer** (CDU: 1949–1963), the Federal Republic benefitting from close ties to the United States in particular, experienced the so-called Economic Miracle (*das Wirtschaftswunder*) which allowed it to recover swiftly from the ravages of the war. Meanwhile, Adenauer's counterpart in the German Democratic Republic, Walter Ulbricht, brutally quelled a popular workers' uprising (on June 17, 1953: the boulevard through the *Tiergarten* in Berlin is named to remember this event) and undertook construction of the Berlin Wall (see pg. 59 of the XXL Glossary, Volume 1), effectively sealing the division of Berlin and the two German states.

Willy Brandt, Chancellor from 1969 until 1974 representing the Social Democratic Party (SPD), ushered in a new period in German foreign relations by acknowledging the GDR as a state and not merely a Soviet occupation zone. This allowed for establishment of formal relations not just with East Germany but with other Eastern bloc states. His visit to the Warsaw Ghetto, where he knelt before the memorial there, became a visual symbol of his *Ostpolitik* (politics of the East), intended to diffuse tensions between the two sides. For his policy of "reconciliation between old enemies", Brandt was awarded the Nobel Peace Prize in 1971.

Helmut Schmidt, Chancellor from 1974 to 1982 (SPD), tackled numerous domestic problems, including the terrorism of the RAF (*Rote Armee Fraktion* – Red Army Faction). Economic troubles, coupled with issues of security led to the dissolution of the coalition between the SPD (Social Democrats) and the FDP (Free Democrats – the liberals) and allowed the CDU to gain the majority.

In 1982, **Helmut Kohl** of the CDU (Christian Democratic Union, the conservative party), began his 16-year tenure as Chancellor. He oversaw the controversial stationing of U.S. and NATO Pershing II missles to counter the Soviet SS-20 missles stationed in East Germany. In one of history's more pronounced ironies, the same Chancellor who so visibly opposed the military maneuvers on the opposite side of the Iron Curtain would eight years later oversee the reunification of the two German states and argue before the Soviet government for Germany's rights to sovereignty.

Self-Evaluation

$\smile\smile$ $\smile$ $\cdot\cdot$

When listening, I can understand (Hören)

– instructions: *Zum Schluss muss man die Fahrkarte stempeln. /*
Reservieren Sie dort die Tickets.

In written texts, I can understand (Lesen)

– information in tourist brochures: *Öffnungszeiten Dom: Montag bis Freitag …*

I can produce the following oral structures (Sprechen)

– asking for information at a tourist office or at a hotel reception desk:
Ich möchte heute eine Stadtführung machen. / Haben Sie ein Zimmer frei?
– state my obligations: *Ich muss mein Zimmer aufräumen.*
– give advice or make a recommendation: *Trink doch ein Glas Wasser …*

I can produce the following written texts (Schreiben)

– fill out a hotel registration form: *Name, Adresse, Ankunft …*

Kursbuch	Textbook
Seite 28	**page 28**
das Auge, -n	eye
gesund	healthy
die Gesundheit (nur Singular)	health
krank	sick
die Krankheit, -en	sickness, illness
der Mensch, -en	human, person
die Papageienkrankheit (nur Singular)	*parrot illness*
die Psittakose, -n	*psittacosis (parrot fever)*
die Schmerzen (nur Plural)	pains, aches
der Tierarzt, ÷e	*veterinarian*
tot	dead
der/die Tote, -n	*the dead one*

Seite 29	**page 29**
gefährlich	dangerous
husten	to cough
nervös	nervous
nun	now
sollen	should
der Trick, -s	*trick*
untersuchen	to examine
vorsichtig	careful

Seite 30	**page 30**
der Arm, -e	arm
der Bauch, ÷e	belly, abdomen
das Bein, -e	leg
dick	fat, swollen
der Finger, -	finger
der Fuß, ÷e	foot
gegen	against, versus
der Hals, ÷e	throat
die Hand, ÷e	hand
der Kopf, ÷e	head
der Mund, ÷er	mouth
die Nase, -n	nose
das Ohr, -en	ear
der Rücken, -	back
schlimm	painful
weh·tun	to hurt

Seite 31	**page 31**
der/die Arme, -n	poor (person)
euer/eure	your (plural: possessive of *ihr*)
die Kopfschmerzen (nur Plural)	headache
mitzeichnen	*to draw along with someone else*
das Monster, -	*monster*
das Monsterspiel, -e	*monster game*
die Ohrenschmerzen (nur Plural)	earache

schmutzig	dirty
sein/seine	his (possessive of *er* and *es*)
weg sein	to be away

Seite 32	**page 32**
der Anrufer, -	*caller (on phone)*
die Empfehlung, -en	*recommendation*
das Fieber (nur Singular)	fever
das Gesundheitsproblem, -e	*health problem*
das Gesundheitstelefon, -e	*ask-a-nurse hotline*
die Halsschmerzen (nur Plural)	sore throat
öffnen	to open
der Rat (nur Singular)	*advice*
rausgehen	*to go out*
die Rückenschmerzen (nur Plural)	backache
so viel	so much
die Tablette, -n	tablet, pill
zu dick	too fat/heavy

Seite 33	**page 33**
der Absender, -	sender
die Anfrage, -n	*inquiry*
die Anrede (nur Singular)	*form of address (such as the opening of a letter)*
der Aquafitness-Kurs, -e	*water exercise class*
die Auskunft, ÷e	information
aus·probieren	*to try out*
besondere	special
der Betreff (nur Singular)	*subject (of a letter)*
bieten; er hat geboten	to offer
dagegen	*here:* to alleviate that
das Datum, Daten	date
die Depression, -en	*depression (clinical)*
deprimiert	*depressed*
donnerstags	Thursdays
der Elan (nur Singular)	*pep, verve, energy*
der Empfänger, -	recipient
die Entspannung, -en	*relaxation*
das Extra, -s	*extra*
fit	fit, in shape
genießen; er hat genossen	to enjoy
das Gruppenseminar, -e	*group seminar*
im Voraus	in advance
inklusive	including
der Kontakt, -e	contact
das Konzentrationsproblem, -e	*problem with concentration*
das Lach-Yoga (nur Singular)	*laugh yoga*
das Lernproblem, -e	*learning difficulty*
die Lichttherapie, -n	*light therapy*
die Massage, -n	*massage*
der Optimismus (nur Singular)	*optimism*
das Quellwasser, -	*spring water*
der Reiterhof, ÷e	*riding stable*
die Reitstunde, -n	*riding instruction*
die Reittherapie, -n	*riding therapy*
die Sauna, -s/Saunen	*sauna*
die Schlafstörung, -en	*sleep disturbance*
Sehr geehrte Damen und Herren	Ladies and Gentlemen

die Situation, -en	situation
starten	to start
das Tagesseminar, -e	*day-long seminar*
die Therapie, -n	*therapy*
das Thermalbad, ̈er	*hot bath (usually from hot springs)*
der Treffpunkt, -e	*meeting point*
die Unterschrift, -en	signature
versuchen	to try, attempt
vor Ort	*on location*
die Winterdepression, -en	*seasonal affective disorder*
das Wochenendseminar, -e	*weekend seminar*

Seite 34   page 34

absagen	*to cancel (an appointment)*
ändern	to change
der Anruf, -e	phone call
der Arzttermin, -e	*doctor's appointment*
bis später	until later, see you/talk to you later
der Doktor, -en	doctor (academic title)
der Freitagnachmittag, -e	Friday afternoon
der Friseur, -e	hairdresser
der Friseurtermin, -e	*hair appointment*
der Massagetermin, -e	*massage appointment*
die Masseurin, -nen	*masseuse*
das Rollenspiel, -e	*role-play*
die Rückenmassage, -n	*back massage*
die Terminvereinbarung, -en	*setting up an appointment*
vereinbaren	to agree to something
verschieben; er hat verschoben	to delay, push back
vorbei·kommen; er ist vorbeigekommen	to stop by

Seite 35   page 35

die Bauchschmerzen (nur Plural)	abdominal pains, stomachache
die Handlungsanweisung, -en	*instructions for activity*

Seite 36   page 36

da ist alles dran	*it has everything it needs*
das Körperteil, -e	*body part*
die Redewendung, -en	*turn of phrase, figure of speech*
die Rolle: eine Rolle spielen	role; to play a role

Seite 37   page 37

hinein·stecken	to stick in
hinter	behind
die Wand, ̈e	wall

Arbeitsbuch   Workbook

Seite 102   page 102

die Aufgabe, -n	exercise
ein·ordnen	*to put in order*
der Zahn, ̈e	tooth

Seite 104   page 104

Armenien (nur Singular)	*Armenia*
der Kanadier, -	*Canadian*
Nordamerika (nur Singular)	*North America*

Seite 106   page 106

der Tennislehrer, -	*tennis instructor*

Seite 108   page 108

her·hören	to listen
der Multivitaminsaft, ̈e	*multivitamin juice*

Seite 109   page 109

das Familienhotel, -s	*family hotel*
die Kinderermäßigung, -en	*children's discount*
das Skiparadies, -e	*skiing paradise*
der Skiurlaub, -e	*skiing vacation*

1   The possessive article *mein, dein, ...* (Possessivartikel)

examples   *Dein Fuss ist ja ganz dick!*   Your foot is really swollen!
Oh, Ihre Hand sieht ja schlimm aus!   Ooh, your hand looks painful!
Koko ist krank. Sein Kopf ist ganz heiß.   Koko is sick. His head is really hot.

For every personal pronoun, there is a corresponding possessive article. In Chapter 2, you have already seen how the articles *mein* and *Ihr* correspond to *ich* and *Sie*. Now let's look at the complete paradigm:

singular

1st person	2nd person	3rd person		
		m	n	f
ich	*du*	*er*	*es*	*sie*
mein	*dein*	*sein*	*sein*	*ihr*

plural

1st person	2nd person	3rd person/formal address
wir	*ihr*	*sie/Sie*
unser	*euer*	*ihr/Ihr*

The 3rd person singular has one form for the masculine *(sein)* and another for the feminine *(ihr)*. The masculine form is also that for the neuter, while the feminine form is also that for the plural.
Just as there are three pronouns *sie*, the possessive article *ihr* appears in three roles: both feminine singular and 3rd person plural use it in the lower case, while the formal *Sie* uses it capitalized (*Ihr*). Again, context makes clear what each form refers to.

		m	n	f	pl
nominative	*Wo ist/sind denn*	*mein Pass*	*mein Handy*	*meine Fahrkarte*	*meine Schlüssel?*
accusative	*Hast du*	*deinen Pass*	*dein Handy*	*deine Fahrkarte*	*deine Schlüssel?*

Just like other articles, possessive articles show a noun's gender, case and number. The endings are identical to those of *ein* (except in the plural) and *kein*.

examples   *Euer Gepäck ist noch im Auto.*   Your luggage is still in the car.
Hier bitte, eure Eintrittskarten.   Here you are, your admission tickets.

The possessive article *euer* loses the *-e-* before the *-r* whenever an ending is added.

2   The modal verb *sollen (Modalverb)*

examples   *Der Arzt hat gesagt, ich soll drei Tabletten nehmen.*   The doctor said I should take three tablets.
Frau Meier, Sie sollen bitte Ihren Mann anrufen.   Mrs. Meier, you should call your husband.

The modal verb *sollen* corresponds directly to the English "should" or "supposed to".

examples   *Ich muss am Wochenende arbeiten.*   I have to work on the weekend.
Ich soll am Wochenende wieder arbeiten.   I should work again on the weekend.
Herr Shalabi muss im Hotel den Ausweis abgeben.   Mr. Shalabi has to turn in his ID at the hotel.

While *müssen* indicates duty or requirement of something, *sollen* leaves open the possibility that it might not be done. For that reason, legal requirements are expressed with *müssen* and never with *sollen*.

examples   *Vergiss den Termin beim Arzt nicht!*   Don't forget the doctor's appointment!
– Wie bitte?   – What?
Du sollst den Termin beim Arzt nicht vergessen!   You shouldn't forget the doctor's appointment!

With *sollen*, an imperative can be restated or reinforced.

examples   *Sollen wir mal wieder ins Kino gehen?*   Shall we go to the movies again?/
Do you want to go to the movies again?

Soll ich Sie mitnehmen?   Shall I take you along?/Do you want to come with?

Soll ich dir helfen?   Shall I help you?/Do you want my help?

Just like in English, *sollen* can be used to propose something. It then serves as the equivalent of "shall" in polite requests.

examples   *Hat Brigitte wieder Kopfschmerzen?*   Brigitte has a headache again?
Dann soll sie (doch mal) zum Arzt gehen.   Then she really should go to the doctor.

In such cases as this one above, *sollen* is used to make a recommendation for a person not in the conversation. In this function, it is often accompanied by the particles *doch* and/or *mal*.

3   The modal verb *sollen* in sentences

examples   *Wir sollen zu Hause bleiben.*
Ich soll morgen um 9 Uhr im Büro sein.
Peter soll für ein Jahr nach Venezuela gehen.

Like other modal verbs, *sollen* functions as the first part of the verbal bracket: it is conjugated in the second position and the dependent infinitive sits at the end of the clause. This infinitive can be omitted only if context makes the meaning clear without it.

Forms and Structures

examples *Der Arzt sagt, du sollst drei Tabletten* | The doctor says you should take three tablets
am Tag nehmen. | a day.
Herr Thomsen hat gesagt, du sollst morgen | Mr. Thomsen said you should come to his office
um 9 Uhr in sein Büro kommen. | tomorrow at 9.

Note that, while in English we simply continue from one clause to the next ("the doctor says", "you should take"), German requires a comma between the two.

Now that you have learned *sollen*, you have all the modal verbs save for one, and the *möchte*-forms stem from that last modal. Here then is a summary of modal verbs to date:

All the forms:

infinitive	können	dürfen	müssen	sollen	wollen	„möchten"
ich	kann	darf	muss	soll	will	möchte
du	kannst	darfst	musst	sollst	willst	möchtest
er/es/sie	kann	darf	muss	soll	will	möchte
wir	können	dürfen	müssen	sollen	wollen	möchten
ihr	könnt	dürft	müsst	sollt	wollt	möchtet
sie/Sie	können	dürfen	müssen	sollen	wollen	möchten

Their functions:

können
capability | *Können Sie Englisch (sprechen)?*
possibility | *Kannst du morgen kommen?*
permission | *Kann ich mal deinen Stift haben?*
request | *Können Sie das bitte erklären?*

dürfen
permission | *Darf ich Sie etwas fragen?*
prohibition | *Hier darf man nicht parken.*

müssen
obligation | *Als Taxifahrer muss man auch nachts arbeiten.*
necessity | *Ich muss noch einkaufen.*
recommendation | *Sie müssen unbedingt mal einen Ausflug nach New York machen.*

sollen
obligation | *Wir sollen das Wörterbuch mitbringen.*
proposal | *Soll ich einen Tisch reservieren?*
recommendation | *Dein Bruder ist arbeitslos? Dann soll er Deutsch lernen!*

wollen
desire | *Ich fahre in die Stadt. Wollen Sie mitfahren?*
intention | *Wir wollen einen Tanzkurs machen.*

„möchten"
desire | *Marc möchte ein Praktikum machen.*
request | *Ich möchte (bitte) eine Cola.*

4 **What happened? Summarize in English.**

A German friend visiting the United States needs to see a doctor but doesn't speak English. Summarize what your friend says in English for the doctor.

Mein Hals tut seit drei Tagen weh und ich <u>My friend says that</u> ....

habe starke Kopfschmerzen, mein Kopf ist ....

auch ganz heiß. Außerdem huste ich viel, ich ....

habe die ganze Nacht nicht geschlafen. Jetzt ....

habe ich auch noch Bauchschmerzen bekom- ....

men. Ich habe gar keinen Appetit mehr. ....

5 **What did the doctor say? Summarize in German.**

Now tell your friend what the doctor said.

You need to stay home for a few days *Der Arzt sagt, du* .... *ein paar* ....

and rest. Drink lots of water. I'm going ....

to prescribe some pills for the pain. ....

Take one a day. And don't smoke until ....

you're feeling better. ....

6 **Translate into German.**

a Where am I supposed to sign? .... ?

– Here, please. ....

b Look, my leg is all swollen! ...., ... *ja ganz* ....

– Should we go to the doctor? .... ?

c Do you have your driver's license with you? .... *dabei* ?

– I don't have a driver's license. ....

d How is Edward doing? Does he still ....

have a backache? .... *noch* .... ?

– Yes, still. He can't play sports. ....

Listening and Pronunciation

The consonant <h>

hast   hier   Hund

When <h> appears at the beginning of a word or syllable, it is pronounced just like the English <h>.

Remember, though that if <h> appears after a vowel or at the end of a syllable, it is silent and only serves to make the preceding vowel long *(woh-nen, Füh-rung, geh)*.

Pronunciation of initial vowels

heute Abend   ●   *in Europa*

Vowels at the beginning of German words are not linked to the sound at the end of the word before. There is a slight break, or pause, before the vowel beginning the second word is pronounced. This same break, called a glottal stop, also occurs between syllables of compound words where the second syllable begins with a vowel:

Wochenende   ●   *Personalausweis*

Getting It All Down

Understanding advertisements

Very often, information provided in written advertisements relies on vocabulary drawn from English or, to a lesser degree, other languages such as French. Taking the time to look for such cognates can increase your understanding tremendously. Often, sounding out what look like German words exposes the underlying roots in the original; you can hear it before you can see it.

Learning new words and expressions

One way of practicing new vocabulary is to build a game of "language dominoes". On small cards, note one half of a word or phrase, and put the concluding half on another. This allows you not only to reconstruct words and phrases in a fun way, but also allows you to share the fun with others, including native speakers, whose use of those phrases will help to imprint on your memory.

Familiarity and Understanding

Morgens Fango, abends Tango

The German system of medical insurance forms a major part of the social support system. Practically the entire population is insured; about 88% of Germans participate in state health insurance, while 9% voluntarily – and at a higher price – participate in private insurance.

The first group participate in programs offered through over 300 insurance companies, where premium costs are divided between employers and employees. In contrast to the U.S. system of health insurance, co-payments are usually far less and are only charged per quarter instead of per visit, and there are no preferred provider networks. What the two systems do share, however, are rapidly escalating costs and the scramble at all levels of government and management to control them.

Another typical aspect of German/Austrian/Swiss medicine is what they call *Kur*. There are towns all over with the word *Bad* as part of their names, and these are localities that usually have or have had natural hot springs, which are widely believed to have curative powers. It is not at all unusual for medical professionals to prescribe a stay at a *Kur* (health spa), located in one of these so-called *Kurorte*, to take the waters as treatment for rheutamic, post-operative or degenerative conditions. Some places, such as Davos in Switzerland, are also well-known for their clean air which then helps in recuperation from respiratory ailments.

Elderly patients especially appreciate and respond to the calm environments and gentle care. There are also usually evening programs that provide entertainment, relaxation and diversion. Concerts and dances are often part of the agenda.

Until recently, more than 300 such localities provided this care, but skyrocketing costs have drastically reduced demand. In its stead, many younger people particularly are choosing instead to book a so-called *Wellness-Urlaub*, combining tourism with the traditional benefits and treatments of *Kur*.

From "ow" to *"aua"*
The German exclamation for pain (what we call "ow" or "ouch") is *aua* or *autsch* (the latter stemming from the English).

Historical Fragments

The Nazi regime, World War II and the Holocaust

When Adolf Hitler was named Chancellor on January 30, 1933, no party held a majority in the *Reichstag* (parlament). Nevertheless, he was able to quickly and legally seize power in Germany. On February 28, 1933, the *Reichstag* building burned (known in German as *der Reichstagsbrand*). Hitler claimed that this desecration proved the threat that opposing parties posed to the *Reich* and used the occasion to dissolve the parliament and thus eliminate his political enemies, in particular the Social Democrats and Communists. Other parties voluntarily resigned while challengers within the Nazi Party were eliminated, and by 1934, Hitler had achieved absolute control over Germany. One particulary enduring symbol of Hitler's rule was the SS (*Schutzstaffel* – the Elite Guard) which functioned above the law, carried out Hitler's policies and also built the infamous network of concentration camps. Over 500,000 Germans fled into exile, among them many artists, writers and scientists.

In spite of all the brutality and eradication of basic rights, the Nazis managed, by building a war-based industrial economy, to overcome the economic oppression that had followed Germany's defeat in the First World War. Grateful for jobs and a chance at a "normal" life, many Germans tolerated or even celebrated Hitler's rule. One of the Nazis' primary objectives, and hence the military-industrial complex that turned the economy around, was war against the nations of Eastern Europe. According to Nazi ideology, Slavs, Communists and Jews were to blame for all of the world's troubles. The Nazis sought to expand the Northern, Aryan race (their own), eradicate other, "inferior" races, and acquire more territory for their empire, the Third Reich, that would then last 1000 years.

The Second World War began when Germany invaded Poland. Great Britain and France then declared war on Germany in support of Poland, thus bringing Hitler's wrath upon them. The *Blitzkrieg* (lightning war) raged across France and rained bombs upon major British cities. All of Germany's neighbors to the north and east were invaded and occupied. The hatred and persecution of the Jews throughout Germany and the occupied territories then turned to genocide. During the Holocaust, 6 million Jews were killed. Additionally, 4 million prisoners of war, convicts, homosexuals and gypsies were exterminated. These deaths came along with the over 20 million casulaties of military combat. In all, the Nazi ideology and its political and military practice carried an unimaginable price.

Self-Evaluation

☺ ☺ ☺

When listening, I can understand (Hören)

– advice and recommendations: *Geh doch mal wieder ins Kino. / Mein Mann soll jeden Tag drei Tabletten nehmen.*

– appointment requests, changes, and cancellations

In written texts, I can understand (Lesen)

– brief advertisements about health treatments, yoga, dance classes, etc.

– other expressions and phrases: *Müssen Sie Ihre Nase überall hineinstecken?*

I can produce the following oral structures (Sprechen)

– making suggestions: *Trink doch ein Glas Wasser.*

– requesting information: *Was heißt/bedeutet …? Können Sie das bitte erklären?*

– describing ailments: *Ich habe Kopfschmerzen. / Mein Bauch tut weh.*

– requesting an appointment: *Ich brauche einen Termin.*

I can produce the following written texts (Schreiben)

– a letter requesting further information about a vacation package at a hotel

Kursbuch	Textbook

Seite 38 — page 38

ab·holen	to pick up
die Bäckerei, -en	bakery (bread)
der Buchladen, ̈	*bookstore*
der Flughafen, ̈	airport
der/die Fremde, -n	*foreigner*

Seite 39 — page 39

| verlieren; er hat verloren | to lose |

Seite 40 — page 40

die Buchhandlung, -en	*bookstore*
der Bus, -se	bus
dahin	*to there*
daneben	next to it
fliegen; er ist geflogen	to fly
das Flugzeug, -e	airplane
geradeaus	straight ahead
in der Nähe	in the vicinity
die Nähe (nur Singular)	vicinity
die Polizei (nur Singular)	police (department)
die Post (nur Singular)	mail (also short for post office)
rechts	right (direction)
die S-Bahn, -en	rapid transit train (operated by German Rail)
die Straßenbahn, -en	streetcar, light rail
das Taxi, -s	taxi
die U-Bahn, -en	rapid transit train (operated by municipal authority)
das Verkehrsmittel, -	*means of transportation*
weiter·gehen; er ist weitergegangen	to continue, to move along
wie weit	how far
zu Fuß	on foot
der Zug, ̈e	train

Seite 41 — page 41

die Ampel, -n	traffic light
die Apotheke, -n	dispensing pharmacy, chemist
die Bank, -en	bank
der Baum, ̈e	tree
die Bushaltestelle, -n	bus stop
das Krankenhaus, ̈er	hospital
liegen; er hat gelegen	to lie (be lying down)
der Lkw, -s	truck, lorry
neben	next to
der Parkplatz, ̈e	parking place

Seite 42 — page 42

| am besten | the best |
| die Ecke, -n | corner |

das Schreibwarengeschäft, -e	paper goods store
das Stadttheater, -	city theater
um die Ecke	around the corner
weit	far
wohin	where to, whither

Seite 43 — page 43

ab·fliegen; er ist abgeflogen	to depart (by plane)
der Abflug, ̈e	*flight departure*
an·kommen; er ist angekommen	to arrive
die Ankunft (nur Singular)	arrival
der Ausgang, ̈e	exit
aus·steigen; er ist ausgestiegen	to alight, disembark, get out of a vehicle
die Durchsage, -n	announcement (in a public place)
ein·steigen; er ist eingestiegen	to board, get in a vehicle
der Fahrplan, ̈e	travel schedule
die Flugnummer, -n	*flight number*
der/die Jugendliche, -n	youth, young person
pünktlich	punctual, on time
das Reisebüro, -s	travel agency
der Schalter, -	counter (for buying tickets)
um·steigen; er ist umgestiegen	to change vehicles
die Verspätung, -en	delay
wie oft	how often
zurück·kommen; er ist zurückgekommen	to come back

Seite 44 — page 44

ab·fahren; er ist abgefahren	to depart
der Anschluss, ̈e	connection
der Bahnsteig, -e	train platform
da drüben	over there
da hinten	back there
da oben	up there
da vorne	up there in front
drüben	over there
der Eingang, ̈e	entrance
das Gleis, -e	track
hin und zurück	round trip (there and back)
hinauf	up (directional)
hinten	in the back
der Imbiss, -e	*snack stand*
der Kiosk, -e	kiosk
die U-Bahn-Station, -en	*U-Bahn station*
unten	below
zurück	back

Seite 45 — page 45

da unten	over there, down below
ebenso	just as
das Flugticket, -s	*plane ticket*
lokal: die lokale Präposition	*locational: preposition of location*
nach links	to the left

nach rechts	to the right
die Orientierung, -en	*orientation*

Seite 46 | **page 46**

vorbei·gehen; er ist vorbeigegangen	to go past

Seite 47 | **page 47**

hinauf·gehen; er ist hinaufgegangen	to go up
hinein	in (directional)
noch mal	once again
der Refrain, -s	*refrain*
ziemlich	*pretty (adverb)*

Arbeitsbuch | **Workbook**

Seite 114 | **page 114**

holen	to fetch
das Kreuzworträtsel, -	crossword puzzle
das Medikament, -e	medication

Seite 117 | **page 117**

das Aspirin (nur Singular)	*aspirin*

Seite 118 | **page 118**

der Stichpunkt, -e	*bullet point, outline point*

Seite 119 | **page 119**

der Stresstag, -e	*stressful day*

Seite 120 | **page 120**

der Informationsschalter, -	*information desk/counter*
das Menü, -s	*menu*

Seite 121 | **page 121**

übrigens	by the way

Forms and Structures

1 The preposition *mit* + dative *(Präposition: mit)*

examples   *Meine Kinder fahren **mit dem Bus** in die Schule.*   My children go by bus to school.
*Kann man zum Thyssen-Museum **mit der U-Bahn** fahren?*   Can you get to the Thyssen Museum on the subway?

When traveling by vehicle, German requires the preposition *mit* to designate what kind of vehicle. The corresponding verb is not *gehen* but *fahren*, or in the case of air travel, *fliegen*.

examples   *Ich **gehe** jetzt zur Post und dann zur Bank.*   I'm going to the post office and then to the bank.

*Willst du **mitfahren**?*   Do you want to go with?
*– Nein danke, ich **gehe zu Fuß**.*   – No thanks, I'll walk.

***Geht** Eva schon in die Schule?*   Is Eva in school already?
*– Nein, sie **geht** noch in den Kindergarten.*   – No, she's still in kindergarten.

*Wir **gehen** für ein Jahr nach England.*   We're going to England for a year.

The verb *gehen* is usually associated with motion on foot. To emphasize the lack of vehicle, the phrase *zu Fuß* is often added.
Just as we use our verb "go" for such expressions as *in die Schule/in die Universität/zum Unterricht gehen*, German does as well. German also has the option of using *gehen* for the general principal of attending, as you will note in the example with Eva.
Be careful when talking about travel! In the last example, it is acceptable to use *gehen*, but for the actual transit, the proper verb is *fahren* or *fliegen*: *Wir fahren nächste Woche nach England.*
Wir fliegen in die USA. The verb *gehen* is appropriate when discussing how long one will stay at the destination.

examples   *Brigitte möchte **mit** Tieren arbeiten.*   Brigitte would like to work with animals.

*Wir kommen **mit den** Kindern.*   We're coming with the children.

The preposition *mit* also has the same meaning as English "with".
Like *seit* and *vor*, *mit* requires dative case.

	m *(der)*	n *(das)*	f *(die)*	pl *(die)*
Fahren Sie	*mit dem Zug*	*mit dem Auto*	*mit der S-Bahn*	*mit den Bussen 27 und 32.*

You learned the indefinite articles of the dative in Chapter 8 *(seit einem Monat/einem Jahr/einer Stunde/– Wochen)*. As you an see from these examples, the definite articles have exactly the same endings and the only new article is of course the plural *(den)*.

2 Locational preposition in response to the question *Wo?* (*Lokale Präpositionen auf die Frage „Wo?"*)

examples

Wo sind Sie geboren?
– *In Mailand. / In der Schweiz. / Im Libanon.*

Where were you born?
– In Milan. / In Switzerland. / In Lebanon.

Wo arbeiten Sie?
– *In einem Supermarkt. / Bei Hueber. / Bei der Polizei.*

Where do you work?
– In a supermarket. / At Hueber. / At the police station.

Wo ist Maria?
– *Im Deutschkurs. / Beim Arzt. / Bei Jörg Fischer. / Bei Frau Hansen. / Zu Hause.*

Where is Maria?
– In German class. / At the doctor. / At Jörg Fischer's (house). / At Mrs. Hansen's (house). / At home.

As you have already seen in Chapter 2, one of the prepositions that can answer the question *wo?* is *in*. It is used in combination with proper geographical names and when referring to general instititutions (but not when using their proper names).
When replying with the proper name of a business, institution or person, *in* is replaced with *bei* (*bei Hueber, beim Arzt, bei der Polizei*).
Using *bei* with a proper name of a person (*bei Jörg Fischer, bei Frau Hansen*) indicates being in their home, or in a work situation, in the person's office.
Note, however, that being **at home** requires the expression *zu Hause*.

When *in* describes someone's or something's location, it requires the dative case, while *bei* always requires the dative case. The forms *in dem* and *bei dem* contract to *im* and *beim*.

	m	n	f	pl
Ich lebe	*im Libanon*	*im Baskenland*	*in der Schweiz*	*in den USA*
Ich war	*beim Direktor*	*beim Touristenbüro*	*bei der Polizei*	*bei den Nachbarn*

examples

Die Kinder schlafen bei Freunden.
Juan schläft mit seinem Bruder zusammen.

The children are sleeping over at friends'.
Jörg sleeps with his brother (in the same room).

Ich wohne bei meinen Eltern.
Ich fahre mit meinen Eltern (zusammen) in Urlaub.

I live with my parents/at my parents' house.
I go on vacation with my parents.

The preposition *bei* always indicates location and never accompaniment. Notice that „*ich wohne bei meinen Eltern*" can be translated to mean that "I live **with** my parents", but only in the sense that we all live in their home, and that is the location. To indicate accompaniment, *mit* is used, either by itself or in conjunction with the adverb *zusammen*.

examples		
*Wartest du **im** Auto?*	Are you waiting in the car?
*Ich habe da **vor** der Schule geparkt.*	I parked in front of the school.
*Die Bank ist **neben** der Post.*	The bank is next to the post office.
*Das Restaurant ist **hinter** dem Bahnhof.*	The restaurant is behind the train station.

The preposition *in* is also used to indicate location within something.
Aside from *in* there are several other prepositions that can answer the question *wo?*
When they function to describe location, they require the dative case:

in	(in, inside of)	*im Bett, in der Tasche, im Wörterbuch*
an	(on, at)	*am Fenster, am Schalter, am Telefon, am Eingang, an der Ampel*
neben	(next to)	*neben Michael, neben der Bäckerei, neben dem Computer*
auf	(on, on top, of, at)	*auf dem Turm, auf dem Parkplatz, auf dem Tisch auf dem Bett, auf dem Balkon*
über	(over, above)	*über den Häusern, über der Stadt, über dem Sofa*
unter	(under, beneath)	*unter dem Schrank, unter unserer Wohnung*
hinter	(behind)	*hinter der Tür, hinter Gerd, hinter dem Haus*
vor	(in front of, before)	*vor dem Hotel, vor den Leuten, vor meinen Augen*
zwischen	(between)	*zwischen zwei Stühlen, zwischen den Haltestellen „Schlump" und „Sternschanze"*

In describing locations, these prepositions correspond very closely to English prepositions. It is important that you visually associate the relation between objects to remember what the prepositions describe.

in expresses "within" when referring to enclosed spaces.
an indicates immediate proximity to vertical objects (*an der Ampel, am Eingang*) but can also indicate contact with an object (*am Telefon, am Schalter*) that *auf* cannot, as *auf* refers to horizontal surfaces (*auf dem Parkplatz, auf der Straße, auf dem Balkon*). Like *in*, *an* also contracts with the article *dem*: *an dem => am.*

The preposition *über* implies no contact with the object (*über der Stadt*) but *auf* does indicate contact (*auf dem Tisch*).

examples		
*Das Auto ist/**steht** vor der Schule.*	The car is (standing) in front of the school.
*Ich bin/**sitze** jetzt im Bus.*	I'm (sitting) in the bus now.
*Michael ist/**liegt** schon im Bett.*	Michael is already (lying) in bed.

When describing someone's or something's position, very often in German (more so than in English) the verb *sein* is replaced by *stehen, sitzen* or *liegen*. Generally, *stehen* is used to describe objects or persons in a vertical position, while *liegen* is associated with a horizontal or reclining position.
Liegen also describes geographical position (*Die Bank ist/**liegt** neben der Post, Isfahan ist/**liegt** im Iran*), and *stehen* is used in expressions such as *Wo (ist) steht das im Text?* (Note that something "stands" or "is" in a text in German, the text does not "say" something.)

3   **Locational prepositions in response to the question *Wohin?***

examples *Wohin fahrt ihr denn in Urlaub?*   Where are you going (to) on vacation?
          – *Nach Italien. / In die Schweiz.*   – To Italy. / To Switzerland.

          Wohin gehst du?   Where are you going?
          – *Nach Hause. / Zum Arzt. /*   – Home. / To the doctor. /
          Zum Training. / Zur Apotheke. /   To the gym. / To the drugstore. /
          Zu Hanna.   To Hanna's (house). / To Hanna.

Some prepositions which indicate a destination or movement toward another point in response to the question *wohin?* are *nach*, *in* and *zu*.

nach is used for proper geographical names without an article *(nach Italien)*. The idiom *nach Hause* indicates home, as in homeward, but not at home.

For proper geographical names with an article, the preposition *in (in die Rioja, in die USA, in den Libanon)* is used. Note that when answering *wohin?* the preposition *in* requires not dative, but accusative case: *Ich bin in der Schweiz geboren (wo?)* but *Ich fahre in die Schweiz in Urlaub (wohin?)*.

When speaking of going to a professional or a particular structure or institution, as well as an event, use the preposition *zu (zum Arzt, zur Polizei, zum Training)*.
In front of a proper name of a person, the preposition *zu* indicates going to that person's house, but can also mean that the subject is going to the point where that person is located at that moment, depending upon the context. Thus, this example *(zu Hanna)* can either mean "to Hanna's house" or "to Hanna".

The preposition *zu* always requires the dative case and it contracts with the singular definite articles of the dative, as you can see in the table below.

	m	n	f	pl
Ich gehe schnell	*zum Frisör* (= *zu dem*)	*zum Auto* (= *zu dem*)	*zur Bank* (= *zu der*)	*zu den Kindern.*

4   **Other expressions in response to the question *Wo?***

examples *Wo bekomme ich Fahrkarten?*   Where do I get tickets?
          Da vorn(e). / Da hinten.   Up front (in the front). / Out back (in the back).

          Entschuldigung, wo ist Gleis 18?   Excuse me, where is track 18?
          Da drüben.   Over there.

          Wo ist hier eine Toilette?   Where is there a restroom here?
          Da unten. / Da oben.   Down there. / Up there.

          Gibt es hier in der Nähe eine Bäckerei? Is there a bakery in the vicinity here?
          Ja, da rechts / da links.   Yes, on the right over there/
                                                      on the left over there.

Locational adverbs can also be used to respond to *wo?* Like in English, such adverbs are often accompanied by gestures signaling direction.

examples	*Fahren Sie **nach links**.*	Turn left.
	*Gehen Sie **nach oben**.*	Go up.

When combined with the preposition *nach*, these adverbs also indicate direction of movement.

Be sure to clarify for yourself that prepositions (which have objects) and adverbs (which stand alone) are not the same and are not interchangeable. The adverbs *oben* and *unten* may look like the prepositions *über* and *unter*, but they do not mean the same thing or function the same way.

5 *Es gibt ... (+ Akk.) / Ist hier ... (+ Nom.) / Da sind ... (+ Nom.)*

examples	*__Gibt es__ hier in der Nähe einen Buchladen?*	Is there a bookstore around here?
	__Ist hier__ in der Nähe eine Apotheke?	Is there a pharmacy around here?
	Ich gehe nicht mehr ins Fitnessstudio.	I don't go to the gym anymore.
	__Da sind__ immer so viele Leute.	There are always so many people there.

The German idiom *es gibt* translates as "there is" or "there are". It is very general, as opposed to the expressions *da ist/sind* which express what is to be found in a particular location. *Es gibt* always requires an accusative complement, while *da ist/sind* always requires a nominative complement.

6 Translate into English.

a *Entschuldigung, wie weit ist es zum Dom?* ....?

– *Das ist gar nicht weit, Sie können* ....

zu Fuß gehen. ....

b *Wo ist das Hotel Novotel?* ....?

– *Es liegt direkt im Zentrum.* ....

7 Translate into German.

a I'm driving to Hamm on Friday. ....

My parents live there. *Da* ....

b I'm going to Karl's house. We want ....

to watch the football game. ....

c Mr. Monroe is on the phone. ....

– Sorry, I don't have any time now. ....

d Excuse me, is there a bus stop around? ....?

– Yes, over there. ....

Listening and Pronunciation

The consonant <z>

Zug ● *zwei* ● *Salzburg*

The letter <z> is pronounced "ts". It sounds like the end of our word "hits" or the middle of "pizza".

Parkplatz ● *sitzen*

There is no difference in pronunciation between <z> and <tz>; both sound like "ts".

Getting It All Down

Tongue Twisters

Tongue twisters (in German, *Zungenbrecher*) are a great way to improve your pronunciation of sounds and different combinations of sounds. Taking the "z" sound as an example: „*Zehn zahme Ziegen zogen zehn Zentner Zucker zum Zoo.*"
There are numerous sites on the internet with collections of tongue twisters for all sorts of sounds. To get the maximum benefit, like with any athletic achievement, it's best to start slow and work up speed. You may even enjoy tracking how your pronunciation evolves along the way.

Schedules and announcements

The best method for improving your ability to find the most important information in a schedule is to practice ahead of time – to prepare for battle, so to speak. Using plane, train or bus schedules on the internet gives you the opportunity to look for information you might need, without the pressure of missing your connection. Searching for local train and bus schedules for any major city in Germany, Switzerland or Austria is a good place to start.

Familiarity and Understanding

Fahrn, fahrn, fahrn auf der Autobahn ...

Even over 30 years later, the *Kraftwerk* hit lives on: "driving, driving, driving on the Autobahn", the monotone mantra of those who revere the German roadway system.
Contrary to popular opinion, it is not permitted to drive as fast as one wishes anywhere on the *Autobahn* network. Over the last 25 years, the preponderance of congestion has not only made it impossible to drive unrestricted in most areas, but for reasons of safety, various speed limits, usually around 120 km/h (about 75 mph) have been instituted and are well enforced.
In terms of geography, the Autobahn system has little in common with the U.S. Interstate System.

Many stretches of Autobahn pass through breathtaking scenery along the Rhine, or through forests and hills dotted with castles, with all historical and natural landmarks clearly designated. Another stretch, loaded with curves, resembles the historic U.S. Route 66 and is outfitted with numerous facilities for the motorcycle riders who favor it. There is also one stretch of *Autobahn* in the Ruhr region of North Rhine-Westphalia that connects 15 cities with major league soccer teams.

Cycling beyond the summer

The bicycle is a regular mode of transportation in all the German-speaking countries for riders of all ages. Germany, Switzerland and Austria all have special bicycle lanes or paths in the sidewalks for their use. Far from just a pleasant activity, cycling is integrated into German transportation and both cyclists and drivers must fully heed the rules of the road, particularly with respect to the other vehicle.

Cycling is not just limited to urban areas, either. Austria, for example, has over 6000 miles of biking paths. One of them stretches 435 miles from Donauwörth, Germany (northeast of Munich), where it passes the Romantic Road, crosses the Alps and stretches to the Adriatic coast of Italy. Such routes are pan-European; the A1 Euroroute, for example, stretches from Calais in France to St. Petersburg, Russia, crossing seven countries. Of the 2175 miles total, 560 pass through Germany.

Tracks on top: Wuppertal's overhead train

The City of Wuppertal in North Rhine-Westphalia has a rather unique mode of public transportation. In the late 19th century, as Wuppertal was growing into a larger city, the need for better public transportation was complicated by Wuppertal's location along the Wupper river, as well as by heavy amounts of groundwater which precluded subway construction. Eugen Langen (a contemporary and collaborator with Gottlieb Daimler) proposed, tested and built a novel solution:

a single-rail, suspended train built 8 to 12 meters (26–39 ft) above the ground and river along a 13.3 km (8.26 mile) route. The rail is supported by pillars from the ground (also in the river) and has been operating continuously since 1901 (except when damaged in World War II). Now a symbol of the city, the *Schwebebahn* transports about 75,000 people a day, traveling at speeds of up to 60 km/h (37 mph).

Langer also built a *Schwebebahn* in Dresden. It is only 274 m (899 ft) long, but it operates as high as 84 m (275 ft) above the surface. It also operates on a pulley system, in contrast to the *Wuppertaler Schwebebahn*, which works on AC power.

Historical Fragments

Between the *Kaiser* and the *Führer*: The Weimar Republic (1919 – 1933)

The First World War ended in Kiel, Germany, when several sailors mutinied against their commanding officers. Kaiser Wilhelm II abdicated and went into exile, and the Republic was declared on November 9, 1918.
The National Assembly of the first German democracy drafted its constitution in Weimar, the seat of German Classicism where Goethe, Schiller and many others had lived and worked. The Republic was in turn named for the historic city of its genesis.
Meanwhile, the Treaty of Versailles that formally ended the First World War required Germany to cede territory to neighboring countries and pay reparations to the victors, imposing considerable hardship on a country already weakened by four years of war.

Domestically, Germany faced fierce and dangerous political fighting between those who remained of the monarchy's beaurocracy and the Social Democrats who, along with the Communists, felt emboldened by the Russian Revolution of 1917. Though parliament was elected, the President of the *Reich* had the power to appoint and seat ministers without consulting the *Reichstag*, a fact which deepened discord and further destabilized the government.

The global financial crisis of 1929 that followed the U.S. stock market crash sent the already fragile German economy into a tailspin, leaving one-third of Germany's population unemployed and destitute. Desperation paved the way for extremists to enter the political fray, among them the National Socialist German Workers' Party – the Nazis. Without winning even a majority in the *Reichstag*, they were still able to form a coalition that effectively forced the President of the *Reich* to name Adolf Hitler Chancellor in January of 1933.

Self-Evaluation

When listening, I can understand (Hören)

– basic directions for going somewhere: *Gehen Sie immer geradeaus!*

– overhead announcements at a train station or airport: *Achtung, eine Durchsage: Herr Fischer kommen Sie bitte zum Ausgang D23. / Passagiere bitte am Nollendorfplatz aussteigen.*

– information at a train station: *Wo ist der Fahrkartenautomat? – Er ist direkt am Bahnsteig. / Muss ich umsteigen? – Ja, in Leipzig.*

In written texts, I can understand (Lesen)

– essential information in travel schedules: *Abfahrt / Ankunft / Umsteigeort*

– directions for going somewhere: *Sie gehen zuerst geradeaus und dann die zweite Straße rechts.*

I can produce the following oral structures (Sprechen)

– requests for information and necessary items: *Entschuldigung, ich brauche eine Auskunft. / Eine Fahrkarte nach Salzburg, bitte.*

I can produce the following written texts (Schreiben)

– an e mail about what I did today: *Heute Morgen bin ich zuerst …*

Kursbuch	Textbook
Seite 48	**page 48**
der Optiker, -	*optician*
die Sonnenbrille, -n	*sunglasses*
Seite 49	**page 49**
behalten; du behältst, er behält, er hat behalten	to keep
die Brille, -n	eyeglasses
dafür	for it
die Reparatur, -en	repair
vor·spielen	*to play, perform*
zunächst	*at first*
Seite 50	**page 50**
das Geburtshaus, ¨er	*house where someone was born*
die Oper, -n	*opera*
die Opernkarte, -n	*opera ticket*
die Reihenfolge, -n	sequence
das Schloss, ¨er	castle
der Spaziergang, ¨e	walk, stroll
das Training, -s	sports practice
Seite 51	**page 51**
ab wann	from what time on
am Apparat	on the phone
der Apparat, -e	apparatus (*here:* phone)
bis wann	until when
der Fotoapparat, -e	camera
funktionieren	to function
halbe Stunde	a half-hour
das Licht, -er	light
die Marke, -n	brand
das Modell, -e	*model*
der Techniker, -	*technician*
die Viertelstunde, -n	*quarter-hour*
Seite 52	**page 52**
an·machen	to turn on, switch on
auf·machen	to turn off, switch off
die Bitte, -n	request
der Bleistift, -e	pencil
die Briefmarke, -n	postage stamp
buchen	to book
der Chef, -s	boss, chief
der Drucker, -	printer
dunkel	dark
das Feuer, -	fire (*here:* a light for one's cigarette)
der Flug, ¨e	flight
die Heizung, -en	heating
der Ober, -	waiter
das Papier, -e	paper

die Rechnung, -en	invoice, bill
das Schreiben, -	letter, correspondence
die Sekretärin, -nen	secretary (female)
die Tür, -en	door
unfreundlich	unfriendly
verschicken	*to send off*
Seite 53	**page 53**
an·schließen; er hat angeschlossen	*here:* to lock to
benötigen	*to require*
die Deutsche Bahn (nur Singular)	*German Rail*
das Display, -s	*display*
das Fahrradschloss, ¨er	*bike lock*
der Fahrradständer, -	*bike rack*
die Gebrauchsanweisung, -en	user instructions
der Informationstext, -e	*informational text*
die Kreuzung, -en	intersection
leihen; er hat geliehen	*to borrow*
los·fahren; du fährst los, er fährt los, er ist losgefahren	to ride off, to drive of
das Verkehrsschild, -er	*traffic sign*
Seite 54	**page 54**
die Autovermietung, -en	*car rental*
die Band, -s	*music band*
bestellen	to order
informieren	to inform
die Jazz-Musik (nur Singular)	*jazz music*
die Live-Musik (nur Singular)	*live music*
das Opernhaus, ¨er	*opera house*
organisieren	to organize
der Rückruf, -e	*call back, return call*
Sehr geehrte Frau ...	Dear Ms. ...
das Stichwort, ¨er	*keyword*
die Telefonansage, -n	*outgoing telephone message*
übernachten	to stay overnight
zurück·rufen; er hat zurückgerufen	to call back
Seite 55	**page 55**
die Aufforderung, -en	*instruction, command*
das Dienstleistungsgespräch, -e	*conversation with service personnel*
formulieren	*to formulate*
der Konjunktiv (nur Singular)	*subjunctive*
Seite 56	**page 56**
das Dampfbad, ¨er	*steam bath*
das Doppelbett, -en	double bed
die Farblichttherapie, -n	*color light therapy*
das Fitnessangebot, -e	*selection of fitness activities and treatments*
die Fußpflege (nur Singular)	*foot care*

das Gymnastikcenter, -	physical therapy center
herrlich	marvelous, exquisite, splendid
die Kosmetikberatung, -en	cosmetics consultation
der Luxus (nur Singular)	luxury
der Märchenkönig, -e	Fairy Tale King
der Reiseplan, ⸚e	travel plan, itinerary
das Romantikhotel, -s	romantic hotel
die Romantik-Suite, -n	romantic suite
der Salon, -s	salon
die Übernachtungsmöglich-	available accommodations
keit, -en	
umgeben; du umgibst, er	to surround
umgibt, er hat umgeben	
das WC, -s	toilet, water closet
das Wellnessangebot, -e	selection of wellness activities and treatments
weltberühmt	world-famous
der Wohnraum, ⸚e	living space

Seite 57 — page 57

die Buchung, -en	booking
die Entfernung, -en	distance
entscheiden; er hat entschieden	to decide
erwarten	to expect
das Frühstücksbuffet, -s	breakfast buffet
der Gast, ⸚e	guest
das Gästehaus, ⸚er	guest house
die Homepage	home page
kostenlos	free of charge
das Mountainbike, -s	mountain bike
nah	near
die Pension, -en	bed and breakfast
der Service, -s	service
träumen	to dream
TV	TV

Arbeitsbuch — Workbook

Seite 124 — page 124

| der Montagabend, -e | Monday evening |

Seite 127 — page 127

| die Kaffeemaschine, -n | coffeemaker |

Seite 129 — page 129

| die Balkontür, -en | balcony door |

Seite 130 — page 130

an·bieten; er hat angeboten	to offer
das Babysitten (nur Singular)	babysitting
der DVD-Player, -	DVD player
das Erlebnis, -se	experience
erledigen	to take care of
das Familienfest, -e	family celebration
das Firmenfest, -e	company celebration
gebraucht	used
das Hifi-Gerät, -e	hi-fi set
das Kinderrad, ⸚er	child's bicycle
das Leihrad, ⸚er	loaned out bike
der Pkw, -s	passenger vehicle
spezialisiert	specialized
der Spezialist, -en	specialist
das Trekkingrad, ⸚er	trail bike
verdienen	to earn
das Zubehör, -e	accessories

Seite 131 — page 131

derselbe	the same (one)
drucken	to print
rechnen	to calculate

Forms and Structures

1 Temporal prepositions: *vor, nach, bei, in* + dative (*Temporale Präpositionen I*)

examples

*Die Tabletten müssen Sie **vor dem Essen** nehmen.*	You have to take the pills before eating.
***Nach dem Frühstück** liest Karl immer die Zeitung.*	After breakfast, Karl always reads the paper.
***Bei der Arbeit** höre ich gern Radio.*	At work, I like to listen to the radio.
*Herr Fischer ist nicht da. Rufen Sie bitte **in einer Stunde** nochmal an.*	Mr. Fischer isn't here. Please call back again in an hour.

In previous chapters, we have already seen that the prepositions *vor*, *nach* and *in* are used not only as indicators of location and destination; they also have temporal, or time-related functions (*Ich habe vor einem Jahr geheiratet. / Es ist zwanzig vor zehn. / Es ist Viertel nach acht. / Im Sommer möchte ich ein Praktikum machen.*).
Just like in English, the German *in* can refer not only to a specific point in time (*im Sommer*), but also to a period of time in the future (*in einer Stunde*).

The preposition *bei* also has a temporal significance. It can indicate something that exists simultaneously with something else (*bei der Arbeit* = at work/while at work, *beim Essen* = during the meal/while eating.

The majority of temporal prepositions in German require the dative case. Among them are *vor*, *nach*, *bei* and *in*.

	m	n	f	pl	
Vor	*dem Feiertag*	*dem Essen*	*meiner Reise*	*meinen Prüfungen*	*rufe ich Sie an.*
Nach	*meinem Geburtstag*	*dem Konzert*	*der Stadtführung*	*den Ferien*	*gehen wir (mal) zusammen essen.*
Bei	*unserem Ausflug*	*dem → **Beim** Abendessen*	*der Arbeit*	*den Hausaufgaben*	*hatte er eine Idee.*
In	*einem Monat*	*einem Jahr*	*einer Woche*	*zwei Monaten*	*ist das Buch fertig.*

2 Temporal prepositions: *bis, ab* (*Temporale Präpositionen II*)

examples

***Wie lange** brauchen Sie für die Reparatur?* – ***Bis** morgen.*	How long do you need for the repair? – Until/till tomorrow.
Wie lange haben die Geschäfte geöffnet? – *Bis 18 Uhr.*	How long are the stores open? – Until 6 p.m.
*(**Ab**) **wann** kann ich den Fotoapparat morgen abholen?* – ***Ab** fünf.*	(After) what time can I pick up the camera tomorrow? – From 5 o'clock on (any time after 5).

The preposition *bis* indicates the end of a certain period of time. We have seen expressions like this before, such as *von Montag bis Donnerstag*, that answer the question *wie lange?*
To indicate a period of time for which there is no fixed end point, the preposition *ab* is used. The corresponding question here is either *ab wann?* or simply *wann?*

3   Polite requests: *Konjunktiv II (Höfliche Aufforderung)*

examples | *Könnten Sie vielleicht den Termin **verschieben**?* | Could you move the appointment back perhaps?
*Könntest du mal den Reparaturservice **anrufen**?* | Could you call the repair service?

*Würden Sie bitte einen Moment **warten**?* | Would you please wait just a moment?
*Würdest du bitte (mal) das Fenster **zumachen**?* | Would you please close the window?

Polite requests are often accomplished using the *Konjunktiv II* of the verbs *können* or *werden*. Often, the words *bitte*, *mal*, and *vielleicht* further soften the tone of the request.

4   Verb prefixes *auf-, zu-, an-* and *aus-*

examples | ***Mach** bitte die Tür **zu**.* | Please close the door.
*Könnten Sie vielleicht das Fenster **aufmachen**?* | Could you open the window, perhaps?

*Machst du jetzt mal den Computer **aus**?* | Are you turning the computer off now?

***Mach** doch mal das Licht **an**.* | Hey, turn the light on.

By learning a handful of verb prefixes, you can begin to expand your vocabulary quickly. The verb *machen*, for example, takes several prefixes to change its meaning: *aufmachen* = to open, *zumachen* = to close, *anmachen* = to switch/turn on, *ausmachen* = to switch/turn off. In the case of these prefixes, their functions as opposites are consistent throughout the language: auf ≠ zu; an ≠ aus.
These same prefixes can be combined with the verb *sein* to indicate the result of those actions:

examples | *Ist das Fenster noch **auf**?* | Is the window still open?
*Nein, es **ist** (schon) **zu**.* | No, it's (already) closed.
*Ist der Computer noch **an**?* | Is the computer still on?
*Nein, er **ist** schon **aus**.* | No, it's already off.

5   The adverbs *noch einmal, wieder, immer noch,* and *gerade*

examples | *Ist Lola da?* | Is Lola there?
*Im Moment nicht. Könntest du vielleicht später **noch einmal/nochmal** anrufen?* | Not at the moment. Could you call again later, perhaps?

Ist die Brille fertig? | Are the glasses finished?
*Nein, tut mir leid. Könnten Sie in einer Stunde **wieder** vorbeikommen?* | Sorry, no. Could you come by again in an hour?

*Arbeitest du **immer noch** im Hotel Astoria?* | Are you still working at the Astoria Hotel?

*Ist **noch** etwas Suppe da?* | Is there any soup left? (Is there still some soup there?)

Würden Sie vielleicht einen Moment warten? | Would you wait just a moment?
*Herr Graf telefoniert **gerade**.* | Mr. Graf is on the phone just now.

To describe a continuing situation or a recurring action, the adverbs *noch einmal, nochmal* or *wieder* are used in German. They have English equivalents in some cases, but not all. Generally, *noch* corresponds to "still" or "yet" in English, and the sense of "still" is emphasized when it is used with *immer (noch immer)*. But it can also mean "again", particularly when paired with *mal* in any form. This is similar to *wieder*, which always translates to "again" in English.

To indicate that an action is going on at the moment, the adverb *gerade* is used.

6   The adverb/particle *erst*

examples   *Kann ich das Auto morgen abholen?*   Can I pick the car up tomorrow?
   *– Ja, aber **erst** nach fünf.*   – Yes, but only after five.

   Frau Schmidt, würden Sie bitte bei der   Mrs. Schmidt, would you please
   Autovermietung anrufen?   call over to the car rental place?
   *– Ja, aber (**zu**)**erst** muss ich das Schreiben*   – Yes, but I have to send this
    hier verschicken.   letter first.

The word *erst* has two distinct meanings: in contrast to *schon* (already), expecting that something is earlier than expected, *erst* can mean "only" in the sense that something is later than expected, where it translates as "just" as well; and it is also the short form of the adverb *zuerst* (first). This adverb should not be confused with the ordinal number *erst-*, an adjective which always has an ending (*erster, erste, erstes* etc.).

7   Translate into English.

a   *Seit wann habt ihr denn den DVD-Player?*   .... ?

  – Seit zwei Wochen.   ....

b   *Könnten Sie den Computer bis*   ....

  nächste Woche reparieren?   .... ?

  – Kein Problem, am Dienstag ist er fertig.   ....

c   *Würdest du bitte mal den Fernseher*   ....

  ausmachen? Beim Abendessen sehe   ....

  ich nicht gern fern.   ....

  – Schade, der Film war interessant.   ....

d   *Wann kann ich Sie morgen anrufen?*   .... ?

  – Morgen Vormittag. Ab 8 Uhr bin ich im Büro.   ....

8   **Translate into German.**

a   Could you please explain this?   .... ?

     – Yes, of course.   ....

b   Where is Andreas?   .... ?

     – In training.   ....

     He has a game on Friday.   ....

c   Could we take a break?   .... *Pause* .... ?

     Yes, but first let's do this exercise.   ....

d   Please close the windows!   .... !

     – But they're already closed!   .... !

Listening and Pronunciation

The consonant cluster <ng>

Finger ● *Wohnung*

The consonant cluster <ng> within the same syllable (not from one syllable to the next, as in *an-geben*, for example) is pronounced as a single sound, just like the <ng> in English.

Getting It All Down

Temporal prepositions

So that you can use the prepositions of time effectively and correctly, try keeping a narrative record of your daily activities in your study journal. Instead of noting the times and activities in a tabular form (i.e., 10:30 – drank coffee) try writing it down in complete sentences (*Von halb zehn bis Viertel vor elf habe ich Kaffee getrunken*). This will allow you to use the different preposition over and over, but to combine them with relevant vocabulary and to practice your *Perfekt* forms as well.

Familiarity and Understanding

Germans of Legend

King Ludwig II is not the only figure in German history to pass into legend. We learned of his legacy in Chapter 4 of the XXL Glossary, Volume 1; here are a few more colorful characters.

Till Eulenspiegel: an unflattering mirror
According to legend, this picaresque figure lived approximately from 1300 to 1350. Many of his pranks consisted of following his superiors' instructions to the absolute letter, leading to the absurd. One such example involved Till, posing as a baker, asking the master what he should bake. When the enfuriated master replied, bake owls and meerkats for all I care!, he did exactly that. Even though the master was livid, his shop sold out of the novelty baked goods instantly. Eulenspiegel also frequently forced those who believed themselves better than others to face their own humanity, such as when he won a bet against a university rector by teaching a donkey to read, or when he "miraculously" healed a hospital full of chronic patients in one day.
The adventures of Till Eulenspiegel have been translated into over 280 languages and immortalized in a Richard Strauss tone poem. As one mark of his popularity, the phrase *Eulenspiegeleien machen* (making Eulenspiegel farce) is used to describe exceedingly literal interpretation. The French word "espiègle" is synonymous with "picaresque".

Klaus Störtebeker: the pirate who shared and shared alike
Legend tells that Störtebeker (ca. 1360–1401) took his *nom de guerre* from his ability to down 4 liters of beer in one gulp; the name Störtebeker means "drain the vessel". Originally hired as a pirate to steal from the Danish navy to supply Sweden with supplies, Störtebeker and others continued after the war, as the *Likedeeler* (those who share equally) to plunder vessels on the North and Baltic seas and divide the plunder among themselves. The Hanseatic League, a merchant union of numerous cities in northern Europe, sent Simon of Utrecht out from Hamburg to stop the *Likedeeler* and on April 22, 1401, Störtebeker was captured near Helgoland in the North Sea. Much of his legend stems from events surrounding his execution shortly thereafter. It is said that he sought mercy for his companions by asking that as many as he could walk past after his beheading be freed. Supposedly, he had already walked headless past 11 of them when a guard tripped his body, and the 11 were executed anyway.

Baron von Münchhausen: the pinnacle of exaggeration
Known as the *Lügenbaron* (Baron of Lies), Karl Friedrich Hieronymus Freiherr von Münchhausen (1720–1797) was given to outrageous exaggeration of his exploits in the Turkish wars and his experiences in Russia. Among his most famous claims, he told how while he was flying into a besieged town upon a cannonball, he changed his mind and in mid-air climbed aboard a cannonball flying in the opposite direction. As entertainment, the adventures of Baron von Münchhausen have been immortalized on film and in books. In a more somber vein, the psychological disorder Münchhausen-by-proxy Syndrome takes the Baron's name as an indicator for patients who seek attention by exceedingly tragic means.

Lorelei: the irresistable song

The nymph Lorelei, sitting on a cliff along the Rhine, combs her hair while singing a song of mourning for her lost love. Barge sailors passing by on the Rhine are so taken by her captivating song that they fail to note the rocks and torrents along the river, and their barges sink. The source of this legend is a rock overlooking the Rhine at a height of 132 m (433 ft.) at one of the most dangerous bends in the river. About 70 years ago, this segment was dynamited to make passage safer for barges and boats, but the statue beneath the cliff of the grieving nymph with her long hair remains.

Heinrich Heine, a noted poet of late German Romanticism, eternalized the figure of the Lorelei in a famous poem which begins: *"Ich weiß nicht, was soll es bedeuten, dass ich so traurig bin..."* (I don't know what it should mean that I am so sad), that Friedrich Silcher later set to music in a song which is well-known to this day. The legend has further been set to music in several operas as well as by the 1980s German pop group Dschingis Khan.

Historical Fragments

The German Reich (1871–1918)

The German Reich (Empire) was founded in 1871 as a powerful military and economic force within Europe. The Reich allied itself with the dual monarchy of Austria-Hungary, a troubled empire; the Balkans in particular became the epicenter of enormous problems for the continent.

Count Otto von Bismarck served as Chancellor to Kaiser Wilhelm I from the Reich's establishment. Domestically, Bismarck managed to enact important social legislation that still leaves its mark on Germany today. To combat the "enemies of the Reich", Bismarck ensured that Parliament, the *Reichstag*, lacked the ability to form a government, keeping this authority in the hands of the *Kaiser* and away from the Social Democrats, the Catholics and the Poles of East Prussia. Bismarck's problems in foreign policy were no less troublesome; internal problems with ethnic minorities led to alliances with neighboring states to maintain somewhat of a "status quo". Bismarck's goal for Germany was to be seen as a senior partner and a nexus in the relations between European states, pushing conflicts away from the geographic center.

In 1890, the elevation of young Wilhelm II to the rank of *Kaiser* changed nearly everything. Wanting to be his own Chancellor, Wilhelm II dismissed Bismarck, failing to recognize his own limitations and inexperience. Beyond the colonies in Namibia (Southwest Africa), Togo, Cameroon, Tanzania, Burundi and Rwanda, that Bismarck had established, Wilhelm II also purchased further, less lucrative islands and outposts and entered into a strategic alliance with Turkey to build the Baghdad Rail, hoping to establish "a place in the sun" for Germany. His efforts to turn Germany into a *Weltreich* (global empire) led to Germany's isolation from the major powers of Britain, France and Russia, and closer ties to Austria-Hungary.

When Archduke Franz Ferdinand, heir to the throne of the Austro-Hungarian Empire, was assassinated in Sarajevo in June of 1914, the Habsburg monarchy declared war on Serbia. Though Germany had no desire to enter the conflict, it was bound by treaty to support Austria-Hungary, while Russia was bound to support Serbia, and in turn, France had to support Russia and England had to support France. Thus, Austria-Hungary and Germany faced bloody and decimating wars on two fronts. In 1917, the United States declared war on Germany and the tide turned. When both the Ottoman and Austro-Hungarian Empires collapsed in October of 1918, Germany's defeat became inevitable. The sailors' mutiny in Kiel reverberated across the entire country, and on November 9, 1918, Parliament proclaimed the "German Republic". The Kaiser was forced to abdicate and immediately went into exile in Holland. After many riots and tremendous upheaval, a National Assembly gathered in the city of Weimar, leading to the establishment of the *Weimarer Republik* ("Weimar Republic").

Self-Evaluation

When listening, I can understand (Hören)

– information given by a tour guide: *Nach dem Mittagessen machen wir eine Stadtrundfahrt.*

– the difference between a polite request and a command

– messages on an answering machine: *Bitte reservieren Sie einen Tisch für sechs Personen.*

In written texts, I can understand (Lesen)

– informational material: *Am Fahrradschloss sehen Sie ein Licht ...*

– notes with requests or orders related to an activity: *Liebe Frau Wagner, Familie Junghans möchte Karten fürs Opernhaus haben.*

– publicity materials for a hotel

I can produce the following oral structures (Sprechen)

– describing technical problems and asking for technical assistance: *Mein Handy funktioniert nicht mehr. Reparieren Sie auch Handys?*

– requesting something cordially: *Könnten Sie bitte das Fenster zumachen?*

– an outgoing announcement on an answering machine: *Hier spricht ... Bitte rufen Sie mich zurück unter ...*

I can produce the following written texts (Schreiben)

– an advertisement offering my services: *Repariere alles, bin besonders spezialisiert auf Radios ...*

Kursbuch	Textbook
Seite 58	**page 58**
der Gürtel, -	*belt*
das Hemd, -en	shirt
die Hose, -n	trousers, slacks, pants
die Jacke, -n	jacket
der Notfall, ¨e	emergency
der Pullover, -	pullover, sweater
das T-Shirt, -s	t-shirt
Seite 59	**page 59**
das Kleidergeschäft, -e	*clothing store*
oh nein	*oh no*
Seite 60	**page 60**
die Bluse, -n	blouse
günstig	affordable, a good buy
klasse	great, excellent
das Kleid, -er	dress
der Mantel, ¨	coat
der Rock, ¨e	skirt
Seite 61	**page 61**
die Bratwurst, ¨e	*bratwurst*
deutschsprachig	*German-speaking (adjective)*
euch	you all (accusative and dative 2nd pers. Plural)
gehören	to belong to
die Größe, -n	size
ihm/ihr	him/her (dative 3rd pers. sing. pronouns)
ihnen/Ihnen	them/you (dative 3rd pers. plural, 2nd pers. formal pronouns)
die Landschaft, -en	landscape
die Mutti, -s	*mommy, momma*
Seite 62	**page 62**
am liebsten	most favorably (what one likes to do the most)
am meisten	the most
beides	both
das Fahrrad-Rückwärts-Geigen	*riding a bike backwards while playing the violin*
die Geige, -n	*violin*
herzlichen Glückwunsch	congratulations, best wishes
na und?	*so what? What's the big deal?*
nach·machen	*to imitate, impersonate*
der Rekord, -e	record
rückwärts	backwards
schwer	difficult
trainieren	to train
vorwärts	forwards

der Weltrekord, -e	*world record*
zufrieden	satisfied
Seite 63	**page 63**
an·ziehen; er hat angezogen	to put on (clothes), to dress
die Brieftasche, -n	billfold
das Feuerzeug, -e	lighter
das Fundbüro, -s	lost and found office
der Koffer, -	suitcase
schauen	to look
der Schirm, -e	*here:* umbrella
Seite 64	**page 64**
an·probieren	*to try on*
die Baby-Wäsche (nur Singular)	*baby clothes*
das Camping (nur Singular)	camping
die Damenkleidung (nur Singular)	*women's clothing*
die Designer-Mode (nur Singular)	*designer clothing, couture*
die Drogerie, -n	drugstore (without a pharmacy)
die Ehefrau, -en	wife
der Ehemann, ¨er	husband
das Erdgeschoss, -e	ground floor
die Herrenkleidung (nur Singular)	*men's clothing*
die Jeans (nur Plural)	jeans
Jeans-Wear	*jeans wear*
die Kinderkleidung (nur Singular)	*children's clothing*
die Kosmetik (nur Singular)	cosmetics
der Kundendienst, -e	*customer service*
die Kundentoilette, -n	*customer restroom*
die Mode-Boutique, -n	*fashion boutique*
das Obergeschoss, -e	*upper floor*
die Schreibwaren (nur Plural)	*paper goods and writing implements*
stehen; er hat gestanden	*here:* to look good on someone
das Untergeschoss, -e	*lower level*
das Video, -s	video
zahlen	to pay
Seite 65	**page 65**
das Demonstrativpronomen, -	*demonstrative pronoun*
der Frageartikel, -	*interrogative article*
die Komparation, -en	*comparison*
der Komparativ, -e	*comparative form*
der Positiv, -e	*positive/base form of adjective*
der Superlativ, -e	*superlative form*
Seite 66	**page 66**
das Accessoire, -s	*accessory*
die meisten	the most

die Frisur, -en	*hairstyle*
sich fühlen	to feel (good or bad)
die Krawatte, -n	*necktie*
der Kursteilnehmer, -	*class participant*
der Kurstest, -s	*class test*
die Meinung, -en	opinion
die Menschheit (nur Singular)	*humanity, humankind*
die Mode, -n	fashion
die Modenschau, -en	*fashion show*
die Sandale, -n	*sandal*
die Socke, -n	sock
der Stil, -e	*style*
zusammen·passen	to fit together

Seite 67   page 67

auf·schreiben; er hat aufgeschrieben	to write down
demokratisch	democratic
sich interessieren	to be interested
vorlesen	*to read aloud*

Arbeitsbuch   Workbook

Seite 137   page 137

die CD, -s	CD
jcwcils	for each one
das Kochbuch, ⁻er	*cookbook*
die Spezialität, -en	*specialty*
der Strand, ⁻e	beach

Seite 139   page 139

Belgien (nur Singular)	*Belgium*

Seite 140   page 140

eng	tight, narrow
die Sportkleidung (nur Singular)	*sports clothes*

Forms and Structures

1   Demonstrative pronouns: *der, das, die (Demonstrativpronomen)*

		nominative	
examples	m	*Sieh mal, der Pullover!* *– Ja, **der** ist schön.*	Hey look, that sweater! – Yeah, that (one) is pretty.
	n	*Sieh mal, das Hemd!* *– Ja, **das** ist günstig.*	Look, the shirt! – Yeah, that (one) is reasonable.
	f	*Sieh mal, die Tasche!* *– Ja, **die** ist klasse.*	Look, the purse! – Yeah, that (one) is great.
	pl	*Sieh mal, die Schuhe!* *– Ja, **die** sind toll.*	Look, those shoes! – Yeah, those are great.

Pronouns replace nouns and help us avoid being repetitive. Until now, you have only seen personal pronouns in German (i.e., *der Pullover → er*), but there are demonstrative pronouns as well. German demonstrative pronouns in the nominative and accusative are identical to the definite articles. In speaking, they are usually emphasized slightly more than personal pronouns, and are sometimes accompanied by a gesture (pointing or tilting the head).

		accusative	
examples	m	*Wie findest du den Mantel?* *– **Den** finde ich schön.*	How do you like the coat? – I think that one is nice.
	n	*Wie findest du das T-Shirt?* *– **Das** finde ich günstig.*	How do you like the T-shirt? – I think it's reasonably priced.
	f	*Wie findest du die Bluse?* *– **Die** finde ich klasse.*	How do you like the blouse? – I think it's great.
	pl	*Wie findest du die Fotos?* *– **Die** finde ich toll.*	How do you like the photos? – I think they're fantastic.

You will notice that, in the examples of these pronouns in the accusative case, that the sentences always begin with the demonstrative pronoun. This is very different from English, but for anyone familiar with speech patterns in New York City, you will recognize the pattern: **That** I like. **This one** I don't like. Like the New York affectation (which comes to New York by way of Yiddish), the German pattern always puts the stress on the demonstrative pronoun.

2   The interrogative article: *welcher?* – The demonstrative pronoun: *dieser* (*Frageartikel – Demonstrativpronomen*)

		nominative	
examples	m	*Welcher Mantel gefällt Ihnen denn?* *– Dieser.*	Which coat do you like? – This one.
	n	*Welches Buch gehört dir?* *– Dieses da.*	Which book belongs to you? – This one here.
	f	*Welche Brieftasche gehört Ihnen?* *– Diese.*	Which wallet belongs to you? – This one.
	pl	*Welche Antworten sind richtig?* *– Diese hier.*	Which answers are correct? – These here.

The interrogative article *welcher? (welches, welche)* creates the question of "which". It always agrees with the gender of the noun with which it is used. Very often, the response is then given with *dieser (dieses, diese)*. It is used to differentiate between a selection of items (unlike the demonstrative pronouns *der/die/das* etc. which simply emphasize). Often, forms of *dieser* are paired with an adverb such as *hier* or *da*. Both *welcher* and *dieser* take the same endings that the noun's definite article would have.

		accusative	
examples	m	*Welchen Rock soll ich anziehen?* *– Zieh doch diesen an.*	Which dress should I put on? – Put this one on.
	n	*Welches Hemd soll ich anziehen?* *– Nimm doch dieses.*	Which shirt should I put on? – Take this one.
	f	*Welche Bluse soll ich anziehen?* *– Probier mal diese an.*	Which blouse should I put on? – Try this one on.
	pl	*Welche Schuhe möchten Sie?* *– Diese da.*	Which shoes would you like? – These here.

3 Comparison: *gut, gern, viel (Komparation)*

*Timo tanzt **gut** Walzer aber Salsa kann er noch **besser**. Und **am besten** tanzt er Tango.*	Timo dances the waltz well, but he can do the salsa even better. He dances tango best (of all).
*Er fährt **gern** Fahrrad. Noch **lieber** spielt er Geige. **Am liebsten** macht er beides zusammen.*	He likes to ride bikes. He likes playing the violin even more. He likes doing both together best (of all).
*Das EU-Car-Zentrum zahlt **viel**, die Sportunion in Berlin zahlt **mehr**, aber die IT-Service GmbH zahlt **am meisten**.*	The "EU-Car-Zentrum" pays well, the "Sportunion" in Berlin pays more, but "IT Service GmbH" pays the most (of all).

The modifiers *gut*, *gern* and *viel* have unique comparative and superlative forms.
As an adverb or as a predicate adjective, the superlative is constructed using *am* before the modifier.

4 Verbs: conjugation of *mögen (Verb: Konjugation)*

examples	*Ich*	*mag*	*den grünen Pullover am liebsten.*
	Du	*magst*	*doch Fisch, oder?*
	Er/sie	*mag*	*keine Pop-Musik.*
	Wir	*mögen*	*die Pension „Sissi".*
	Ihr	*mögt*	*doch die Berge, nicht?*
	Sie	*mögen*	*Beethoven, stimmts?*

The conjugation of *mögen* follows the same pattern as other modal verbs; the vowel is completely different in the singular forms, and the 1st and 3rd person singular forms have no ending.

While *mögen* is used with dependent infinitives (*Ich mag gern tanzen.*), it is more frequently seen as the sole verb in the clause. Either way, it is equivalent to the English verb "to like" and can take accusative complements. Note the contrast in structure between *gefallen* used to express liking, whereby the subject is pleasing to the dative complement (*Der grüne Pullover gefällt mir.*), as opposed to *Ich mag den grünen Pullover.*

There are many ways to express likes and dislikes in German, so here is a general overview of what works when (+A = with accusative, +D = with dative):

To express liking:
gern haben (+A), mögen (+A), nett/sympathisch finden (+A)

examples		
Ich habe Timo gern.	I like Timo.	
Ich mag Timo.	I like Timo.	
Unsere Lehrerin finde ich nett/sympathisch.	I think our teacher is nice.	

To express preferences in food and drink:
gern essen/trinken (+A), mögen (+A), schmecken (+D), lecker sein/schmecken

examples		
Ist du gern Kartoffelsalat?	Do you like (to eat) potato salad?	
Mögen Sie Granatäpfel?	Do you like pomegranates?	
Schmeckt Ihnen die Suppe?	Do you like the soup (does it taste good)?	
Der Salat ist/schmeckt lecker.	The salad is/tastes delicious.	

To express aesthetic pleasure:
(gut) gefallen (+D), mögen (+A), gut/hübsch finden (+A), gern (+ Verb)

examples		
Die Tasche hier gefällt mir (gut).	I like the purse.	
Mögt ihr Romantikhotels?	Do you like romantic hotels?	
Findet ihr das Buch gut?	Did you like the book?	
Findest du Astrid hübsch?	Do you think Astrid is pretty?	
Hören Sie gern Jazz?	Do you like (to listen to) jazz?	

5   Personal pronouns in the dative case *(Personalpronomen im Dativ)*

examples			
(ich)	*Die Bluse gefällt **mir**.*	I like the blouse (it is pleasing to me).	
(du)	*Ich muss mit **dir** sprechen.*	I have to speak with you.	
(Timo/er)	*Der Pullover gefällt **ihm** bestimmt.*	He is sure to like the sweater (it will be pleasing to him).	
(Corinna/sie)	*Wie geht es **ihr**?*	How is she?	
(wir)	*Kommen Sie zu **uns**!*	Come to our home (to us)!	
(ihr)	*Wir sind um neun bei **euch**.*	We'll be by you (at your house) at 9.	
(sie/Sie)	*Wie geht es **ihnen/Ihnen**?*	How are you?	

The dative personal pronouns do not always translate literally into English (*wie geht es Ihnen?*). Note that the 1st and 2nd person plural pronouns are identical to the accusative forms.

6 Verbs with dative complements *(Verben mit Dativ)*

*Die Kartoffeln **schmecken mir** nicht.*	These potatoes don't taste good (to me).
*Die Jacke **steht dir** gut.*	The jacket suits you well.
***Passen Ihnen** die Schuhe?*	Do the shoes fit you?
*Die Wohnung **gehört mir**.*	The apartment belongs to me.
*Das Training **gefällt mir** gut.*	I really like the training (it is pleasing to me).
*Sollen wir **euch helfen**?*	Should we help you?

While most verbs take accusative complements, some in German take dative complements. Very often, when translating these verbs into English, there is a sense of *to* or *for* someone or something inherent in them: to taste to someone (*schmecken*), to be pleasing to someone (*gefallen*), to belong to someone (*gehören*), to give assistance to someone (*helfen*). In rare cases, such as *passen* and *stehen*, there is nothing corresponding to English usage.

7 Translate into English.

a *Wie gefallen dir die Schuhe da?*

.... ?

  – Die sind zu teuer.

....

b *Welche Jacke soll ich anziehen?*

.... ?

  – Diese hier, die steht dir gut.

....

c *Harald sieht mit Hemd besser aus.*

....

  – Findest du?

.... ?

d *Welche Farbe magst du am liebsten?*

.... ?

  – Am liebsten mag ich Rot.

....

8 Translate into German.

a Which text are we supposed to read?

.... ?

  – This one here. It's on page 66.

....

b The blouse doesn't fit me.

....

  – The size is wrong. Which size do you

....

  need?

.... ?

c Rex, does that dictionary belong to you?

.... ?

  – No, it's yours (it belongs to you).

....

d Are we going by car?

.... ?

  – I prefer to go on foot.

....

Listening and Pronunciation

Connecting consonants of words in succession

Am Mittwoch
Kommst du aus Salzburg?

In contrast to vowels at the end of one syllable and the beginning of the next (Chapter 10), if a word begins with the same consonant as the one on the end of the previous word, or if the consonants are similar (such as b and p, d and t, g and k) then they are sounded together as one.

Word stress in sentences

Wie findest du die Hose?
Die finde ich klasse.

As mentioned earlier in "Forms and Structures", demonstrative pronouns receive the primary stress in a sentence or phrase.

Ist das dein Vater?   Is that your father?
*Ist das **dein** Fahrrad?*   Is that **your** bike?

Just as we do in English, possessive articles can be stressed to express surprise or confusion.

Getting It All Down

Vocabulary by association

By associating words with other words, we can strengthen our recall of their meaning. There are numerous ways to use such associations as learning tools. One is the word web: start with one word and branch off from it to associate subgroupings or types of the original. An example would be *Kleidung* as a starting point, then drawing rays off from that word in the center to have different groups (*Mantel, Hemd, Hose, Rock, Schuh*) and then branching off from each of those to describe a specific type, or a descriptive word that you associate with it.

Another, more novel but often more effective way to create associations is to find absurd connections between words. This is a very individual way to remember things, but because it has particular meaning to the person using it, it is a powerful tool. Think of an absurd visual image, such as a dog wearing cowboy boots, and generate a statement about it, such as *Die Cowboy-Stiefel passen dem Hund gar nicht, sie sind zu groß!* As funny as the image is, the use of the vocabulary and the structure of the sentence are equally as likely to imprint upon your memory.

Familiarity and Understanding

Saga meets epic: *das Nibelungenlied*

Having slain a fearsome dragon, the hero bathes in the beast's blood, knowing that it will make him immune to injury. But unbeknownst to him, a linden leaf landed on the back of his shoulder, preventing the blood from touching him there, forever leaving Siegfried, the Crown Prince of Xanten, vulnerable in this one spot. So begins his quest to win the hand of Kriemhild, sister of Gunther, the King of Burgundy whose court sits at Worms.

Having slain the dragon and taken the Nibelung treasure, Siegfried attempts to court Kriemhild but to no avail, until Gunther asks Siegfried to help Gunther win the hand of Brünhild, the queen of Iceland. Her superhuman strength can only be defeated by Siegfried, who in his cloak of invisibility is able to make it appear that Gunther is the one subduing her. Brünhild remains suspicious, even years after she and Gunther are wed. Upon Siegfried's marriage to Kriemhild, he presents Kriemhild with the ring and the belt that he took from Brünhild while subduing her for Gunther, and when Kriemhild later taunts Brünhild with the two items, thus begins the chain of events leading to Siegfried's murder (struck by a spear in the one vulnerable spot). Kriemhild's revenge against her brother's court is long, brutal and tragic, leading to the demise of both families.

Das Nibelungenlied, the epic of the Nibelungs, has its roots in early Germanic sagas of the 5th and 6th centuries, and was put to paper around 1200. By the time it was written down (and the author has never been determined), it had melded many aspects of Germanic mythology and folklore with numerous characteristics of English and French medieval epics and is considered one of the cornerstones of medieval German literature. It lives on not only in the written texts (about 11 of which still exist in their entirety, with many others as fragments) but also in Richard Wagner's *Ring der Nibelungen* (Ring Cycle), his four operas based equally upon the *Nibelungenlied* and Germanic and Norse sagas (Kriemhild, for example, never appears in Wagner's operas). There are also film versions of the epic, most notably Fritz Lang's 1924 silent opus in two parts.

The Germanic ideals espoused in the original work have been appropriated over time for political ends. Notably, the mutual support treaty between the German Reich and Austria-Hungary referred to *Nibelungentreue*, the type of loyalty that Siegfried showed Gunther in vanquishing Brünhild. As it was for Siegfried, this loyalty also proved disastrous for Germany. The image of mighty and noble Nordic warriors was also appropriated by the Nazis to propagandize their racist ideology in the 1930s.

The Nibelung saga still lives on in the city of Worms. Every year, a festival commemorates the Burgundians, Siegfried, and the epic tale of their friendship and tragic demise.

Historical Fragments

**Between resignation and national unity:
from the Revolution of March, 1848, till the founding of the Reich, 1871**

Though Germany as a political entity only came into existence in 1871, there had always been a notion of Germany and what it meant to be German. After the French Revolution, the idea of a unified Germany slowly began to spread, though it was hampered by the mostly oppressive structures of the various kingdoms and principalities throughout the territories that were loosely defined as Germany. The growth of democratic and liberal movements eventually led to the revolution of March 1848 and the continued revolt in 1849, but the loyalty of troops to their princes and rulers proved too strong in the face of the still fractious opposition, and the conservative status quo remained. In fact, it was not until 1949 that true democracy had any chance to take root and flourish on German soil. Nevertheless, the politicization of German society had begun with the Revolution of 1848.

In 1862, Otto von Bismarck was Prussia's prime minister, and in his position sought to calm the waves of discontent among the population. One step was the declaration of war upon Denmark, who had ruled the Schleswig and Holstein territories (with significant German minorities) in the north of Germany. Together with its ally Austria, Prussia defeated the Danes in 1864, and both Schleswig and Holstein became Prussian territories. This victory unleashed a wave of nationalistic pride.
Still, Bismarck did not want to allow Prussia and Austria to become allied too closely. Forging alliances with the smaller principalities nearby, Bismarck then declared war on Austria and won, establishing Prussia as the leading power among a union of allied states and paving the way for the *kleindeutsche Lösung* or small-scale German solution.

France, meanwhile, was none too happy to witness Prussia's rise to dominance. Napoleon III declared war on Prussia in 1870. The already allied states of the so-called *Norddeutscher Bund* (North German Federation) were joined by the southern German states and together decisively defeated France. With Prussia's position of power secured, King Wilhelm of Prussia was proclaimed Kaiser of Germany at the Palace of Versailles in France on January 18, 1871.

Finally recognized as a single entity and as a major force on the continent, Germany continued to expand by annexing Alsace and Lorraine, but this, too, would lead to later problems. The issues of political restriction also remained. Oppression continued to drive hundreds of thousands of Germans to emigrate in search of better living conditions, while the liberals who remained were trapped in an impossible struggle for basic rights and freedom of expression, and Bismarck zealously guarded the interests of the ruling class he had fought so hard to unite.

Self-Evaluation

When listening, I can understand (Hören)

– whether someone likes a particular item: *Den Mantel finde ich nicht schön.*

In written texts, I can understand (Lesen)

– simple magazine or newspaper articles: *Ungewöhnliche Berufe / Weltrekord im „Fahrrad-Rückwärts-Geigen"*
– locations of various departments in a department store directory: *Erdgeschoss, Drogerie*
– opinions on fashion

I can produce the following oral structures (Sprechen)

– say whether I like something: *Die Hose finde ich nicht so schön. / Der Pullover gefällt mir nicht.*
– stating that something belongs to me: *Diese Brille gehört mir (nicht).*
– comparing clothing: *Haben Sie den Rock auch in Größe …? / Die Hose passt mir nicht. Sie ist zu klein.*
– stating my personal preferences: *Ich fahre nicht gern Auto. Ich fahre lieber Fahrrad.*

I can produce the following written texts (Schreiben)

– a statement of whether I like something
– a description of my preferences in clothing, food, etc.
– my opinion on the importance of a particular topic

Kursbuch	Textbook
Seite 68	**page 68**
das Boot, -e	boat
der Küchentisch, -e	kitchen table
der Rahmen, -	*frame*
das Zitat, -e	*quote, quotation*

Seite 69	**page 69**
die Bootsfahrt, -en	*boat trip*
das Deutsch-Zertifikat, -e	Certification of Proficiency in German
das Geschenk, -e	gift, present
gratulieren	to congratulate
das Happy End (nur Singular)	*happy ending*
das Paar, -e	pair, couple
überrascht	surprised
das Zertifikat, -e	certificate
zurück·gehen; er ist zurückgegangen	to go back

Seite 70	**page 70**
die Geburtstagsliste, -n	*birthday list*
der Kalender, -	calendar
um·ziehen; er ist umgezogen	to move (from one home to another)
der Wochentag, -e	*weekday*

Seite 71	**page 71**
auf·passen	to pay attention, be careful
eilig: es eilig haben	rushed, to be in a hurry
ein·rahmen	*to frame*
herum·fahren	*to drive around*
der Mist (nur Singular)	*crap, dung; here: shoot!*
na	*ahhhhh, ummm …*
das Ratespiel, -e	*guessing game*
vergessen; du vergisst, er vergisst, er hat vergessen	to forget

Seite 72	**page 72**
denn	(has no meaning, expresses curiosity)
das Ding, -e	thing
sich kümmern	to concern oneself with something or someone
laufen	to run
die Überraschung, -en	*surprise*
unwichtig	unimportant
wunderbar	wonderful

Seite 73	**page 73**
das Abschlussgrillen (nur Singular)	*barbeque to celebrate the conclusion of something*
anschließend	following
der/die Bekannte, -n	acquaintance
Bescheid geben; du gibst Bescheid, er gibt Bescheid, er hat Bescheid gegeben	to provide information, pass word on
das Café, -s	café
das Grillfest, -e	*barbeque party*
der Grund, ¨e	reason
der Hiphop-Kurs, -e	*hip-hop (dance) class*
hoffentlich	hopefully
die Kindertanzgruppe, -n	*children's dance group*
die Kirche, -n	church
das Können (nur Singular)	*ability*
die Sommerpause (nur Singular)	*summer break*
so weit	so far, to this point
der Verein, -e	club, organization
vorbei sein	to be over, past
vorhanden sein	*to be on hand, available*

Seite 74	**page 74**
alles Gute	all the best
der Ausdruck, ¨e	expression
die Besserung (nur Singular)	recuperation, recovery (from illness)
bestehen; er hat bestanden	to pass (a test)
Frohe Ostern	Happy Easter
Frohe Weihnachten	Merry Christmas, Happy Christmas
Frohes Fest	Happy Holiday
der Glückwunsch, ¨e	wish for happiness
die Gratulation, -en	*congratulations*
Gute Besserung	get well
Gutes neues Jahr	Happy New Year
heften	*to attach*
der Kursraum, ¨e	*classroom*
das Lebensjahr, -e	*year of life*
das Neujahr (nur Singular)	New Year
das Ostern, -	Easter
die Prüfung, -en	examination
Schöne Ostern	happy Easter (*variation*)
das Silvester (nur Singular)	New Year's Eve, Hogmanay
umher·gehen; er ist umhergegangen	*to go around*
Viel Erfolg/Glück/Spaß/…	Much success/luck/happiness/fun!
das Weihnachten (nur Singular)	Christmas

Seite 75	**page 75**
die Absage, -n	*cancellation of plans*
die Ordinalzahl, -en	*ordinal number*
die Zusage, -n	*agreement, OK to proceed*

Seite 76 — page 76

auf·wachen	to wake up
erfahren; du erfährst, er erfährt, er hat erfahren	*here*: to learn, find out
golden	*golden*
das Karussell, -s	*carousel*
klingeln	to ring
die Liebesgeschichte, -n	*love story*
die Mittagspause, -n	*lunch break*
der Nikolaus, ⁓e	*St. Nicholas*
der Nikolausbart, ⁓e	*St. Nicholas' beard*
der Nikolausmantel, ⁓	*St. Nicholas' coat*
die Nikolausmütze, -n	*St. Nicholas' cap (miter)*
die Nikolaus-Sachen (nur Plural)	*St. Nicholas things, accessories*
rundherum	*around and around*
der Sack, ⁓e	*sack*
vorweihnachtlich	*pre-Christmas (adjective)*

Seite 77 — page 77

der Christ, -en	*Christian*
das Gebiet, -e	region
die Haustür, -en	house door
heutig	current, what is currently
die Info, -s	*info*
Kleinasien (nur Singular)	*Asia Minor*
lieb	dear
die Nikolaus-Agentur, -en	*St. Nicholas booking agency*
der Nikolaustag (nur Singular)	*St. Nicholas Day*
nördlich	*north*
die Nuss, ⁓e	*nut*
professionell	*professional*
sauer	*here*: in a bad mood
der Schokoladen-Nikolaus, ⁓e	*chocolate St. Nicholas*
sterben; du stirbst, er stirbt, er ist gestorben	to die
der Teller, -	plate
der Weihnachtsmarkt, ⁓e	*Christmas market*
wieder·kommen; er ist wieder- gekommen	to come again

Seite 78 — page 78

der Anlass, ⁓e	*here: event*
die Anweisung, -en	*instruction*
ein·holen	*retrieve*
die Reiseleitung, -en	*travel plan*
die Übersichtstafel, -n	*overview table*
unterschiedlich	*different*
die Wegbeschreibung, -en	*description of how to arrive at a location*
der Zeitungsartikel, -	*newspaper article*

Seite 79 — page 79

aus·sprechen; du sprichst aus, er spricht aus, er hat ausge- sprochen	to express

erfragen	*to ask for (information)*
das Gerät, -e	device
die Pflicht, -en	duty
schriftlich	in writing
zusagen	*to agree to*

Arbeitsbuch — Workbook

Seite 142 — page 142

das Sommerfest, -e	*summer festival*

Seite 143 — page 143

bestimmen	to determine
das Gedicht, -e	*poem*
die Strophe, -n	strophe

Seite 145 — page 145

das Feuerwerk, -e	*fireworks*
die Mitternacht (nur Singular)	*midnight*
der Sekt (nur Singular)	*sparkling wine similar to champagne*
die Weihnachtsfeier, -n	*Christmas party*

Forms and Structures

1 Ordinal numbers: dates *(Ordinalzahlen: Datum)*

examples *Heute ist **der zweite** September.*   Today is September second/the second of September.
*Morgen ist schon **der vierundzwanzigste** März.*   Tomorrow will already be March 24th.

Like English, the naming of calendar dates requires ordinal numbers. Unlike English, however, those numbers need endings.
Ordinal numbers are formed by adding the endings *-te* (up to 19) or *-ste* (from 20 on up). There are only three irregular cases:

eins   –   *der erste*
drei   –   *der dritte*
sieben –   *der siebte*

The number *acht* loses its final *-t* when the *-te* ending is added, avoiding a double T.
acht   –   *der achte*

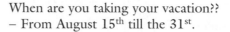

examples *Welcher Tag ist heute?*   Which day is today?
*– Heute ist **der dritte** Mai.*   – Today is the third of May.

Wann hast du Geburtstag?   When is your birthday?
*– Am **achten** Juli.*   – (On) July 8.

Wann machen Sie Urlaub?   When are you taking your vacation??
*– **Vom fünfzehnten bis (zum)** einunddreißig**sten** August.*   – From August 15th till the 31st.

For asking what day of the week it is, the expression *Welcher Tag* (or *Was für ein Tag*) *ist heute?* is used. When answering the question *wann?* the day or date is preceded by *am* (on the), *vom* (from the), *bis* or *bis zum* (until the), and the ordinal number ends with *-(s)ten*. This is correct with days of the week as well (*am Montag, bis zum Sonntag*); even though we would not use an article, German does in these instances.

2 Accusative personal pronouns *(Peronalpronomen im Akkusativ)*

examples

nominative	accusative	
ich	*Er liebt **mich**.*	He loves me.
du	*Soll ich **dich** mitnehmen?*	Should I take you along?
er	*Der Fernseher ist kaputt. Können Sie **ihn** reparieren?*	The TV is broken. Can you repair it?
es	*Das Radio ist noch an. Mach **es** bitte aus.*	The radio is still on. Please turn it off.
sie	*Die Tasche ist teuer, aber ich mag **sie** nicht.*	The purse is expensive, but I don't like it.
wir	*Besuchst du **uns** mal?*	Will you visit us sometime?
ihr	*Ich hole **euch** ab.*	I'll pick you all up.
Sie	*Wir rufen **Sie** an.*	We'll call you.
sie	*Wo sind meine Jeans? Hast du **sie** gesehen?*	Where are my jeans? Have you seen them?

In any event, while it is customary for Germans to begin sentences with demonstrastive accusative pronouns, it is not the norm to begin with an accusative personal pronoun.

Wie findest du den Rahmen?
– Den (Rahmen) finde ich toll! / Ich finde ihn toll. ~~(Ihn finde ich toll.)~~

3   The conjunction *denn (Konjunktion)*

examples

Ich mache gern Sport. Ich will fit bleiben.	I like playing sports. I want to stay fit.
Ich mache gern Sport, **denn** *ich will fit bleiben.*	I like playing sports because I want to stay fit.

The conjunction *denn* indicates a cause, and it joins two main clauses (*Hauptsätze*). Note that when *denn* is used as a conjunction, it is preceded by a comma.

In previous chapters you have learned other coordinating conjunctions (that join main clauses):

examples   *Lisa kommt um vier* **und** *bringt Kuchen mit.*
Gehen wir ins Kino **oder** *möchtest du lieber zu Hause bleiben?*
Marco war krank, **aber** *jetzt geht es ihm wieder besser.*

4   Verbs: conjugation of *werden (Verb: Konjugation)*

examples

Ich werde am Freitag 30!	I'm turning 30 on Friday!
Du wirst aber schnell braun!	You're getting tan quickly!
Sie wird leicht rot.	She becomes red easily.
Wir werden Großeltern.	We're becoming grandparents.
Ihr werdet bestimmt gute Freunde.	You will certainly become good friends.
Sie werden alt.	They're getting old.

You have seen *werden* in its subjunctive form as an auxilliary verb *(Würden sie bitte warten?)* but it also functions as a main verb. It means "to become" and as such can also translate into English in different ways, but always points to the process of becoming something else. ("They're getting old" means that they are becoming or growing old, not that they are acquiring/getting anything.) Complements of *werden* are always nominative.

You will note from these examples that plural forms of *werden* are entirely regular, but the singular forms are quite unique. The verb *werden* is one of the most important in the language, so be sure to commit it to memory right away.

5 **Translate into English.**

a *Meine Frau wird jetzt Direktorin*

an ihrer Schule.

– Herzlichen Glückwunsch!

b *Ich habe gestern deinen Chef*

kennengelernt.

– Wie findest du ihn?

c *Ich lerne gern mit diesem Buch,*

denn es macht Spaß.

– Ja, es ist klasse!

d *Frau Wesel, kommen Sie auch zu unserer*

Feier?

– Ich weiß es noch nicht.

Bitte geben Sie mir bis Montag Bescheid.

6 **Translate into German.**

a What day is it today?

– October 3rd.

b I would like to move my appointment

back.

– Can you come on May 23? It's a Friday.

c Lena is turning 30 on Saturday,

are you guys going to her party?

– Yes, should we pick you guys up?

d Dani can't drive because he drank wine.

– OK, we'll call a taxi.

e Peter has an exam tomorrow but he

hasn't done anything.   *nichts*

– I don't understand him.

Listening and Pronunciation

Intonantion of joined sentences

Ich mache heute ein Fest, ➜ *denn ich habe Geburtstag.*
Heute Nachmittag gehe ich schwimmen, ➜ *oder ich fahre mit dem Fahrrad.*

In the case of sentences joined with conjunctions such as *und*, *denn*, *aber*, or *oder*, the melody of the first phrase neither rises nor falls in comparison to the second, but rather stays level, so that one sentence flows into the next. In this manner, the listener knows that something more is coming.

Trinkst du einen Kaffee ➚ *oder möchtest du lieber einen Tee* ➘ ?

If two questions are linked, the first question intones slightly up, while the second one then intones down.

Getting It All Down

Learning to summarize

When reading texts, take advantage of the fact that your passive knowledge will always be greater than your active knowledge. Instead of getting buried in little details and individual words, read an entire text through all at once. Then, before you get distracted by all that you think you don't understand, summarize quickly, even in English, what you do remember of the text. Don't worry about whether you are right or wrong in your recall. Read it again a second time, still pushing through, no dictionary, no questions. Check your notes from the first reading, see what you can add or subtract to it. Then, after you have first given yourself a chance to use your passive knowledge and become familiar with the text, reach for the glossary or dictionary. Don't translate the text. Just look up enough to summarize the text; write down the main points and essential information.

Familiarity and Understanding

***Oh Tannenbaum, oh Tannenbaum ...* and other holiday customs**

In September and October, shops in the German-speaking countries begin to stock Christmas treats. In addition to the chocolate figures there are assorted baked goods such as *Spekulatius* (a spiced almond cookie) or *Zimtsterne* (literally, cinnamon stars), *Dominosteine* (literally, domino tiles, a double-filled gingerbread cookie), and of course *Christstollen*, a yeast cake with raisins and dried fruits, covered in powdered sugar. By November, Christmas ornaments are available and an orgy of consumer frenzy not unlike that in North America is fully underway.

The reknowned Cologne-born writer Heinrich Böll (1917–1985) wrote a popular satire of German Christmas tradition, *Nicht nur zur Weihnachtszeit* (Not just at Christmastime) in which the narrator's elderly Aunt Milla goes berserk while the family takes down her Christmas tree 40 days after the holiday, and insists that the family hold Christmas every evening. Eventually, family members even go so far as to hire actors to replace them at the festivities and one even becomes a monk just to escape the holiday torture.

Most of the traditions that Americans keep in December come from Germany: the wreath comes from the German *Adventskranz* while the Christmas tree itself comes from the *Weihnachtsbaum*. Most of our cookies stem from the German tradition, and though our well-known and oft-reviled fruitcake comes from England, most Americans find *Stollen (Christstollen)* to be quite enjoyable, if not well known.
One major difference in traditions, however, is December 6, which in Germany, Austria and Switzerland is known as *Nikolaustag*, the day when St. Nicholas fills the boots or socks children set out the night before with treats and surprises (if they have been good that year – bad children get only a tree branch). It is not a work holiday but only exists for the children.

Traditionally, Germans have their own Christmas trees on Christmas Eve (*Heiligabend)* and celebrate with immediate family. *Weihnachten* is then two days long, the 25th and 26th of December. The traditional meal of roast goose and carp was eaten on *Heiligabend*, but as families grow smaller and farther apart in Germany especially, these family feasts are growing less common.

New Year's Eve, or *Silvester* in German, is celebrated very much like in the U.S. with fireworks, noise-makers and toasts at midnight.

In south and west Germany (where Catholicism is prevalent) as well as in German-speaking Switzerland, the season leading up to Lent, known as *Karneva*l, *Fastnacht*, or *Fasching*, is a time of great revelry. The regional traditions vary almost from town to town in some areas, but all begin on *Dreikönigstag* (Epiphany) and end on *Aschermittwoch* (Ash Wednesday) with the high point of the festivities occuring in the days just before the end. It is comparable (though not identical) to Mardi Gras in New Orleans.

Holy week, at the end of Lent, is celebrated much like in the United States, both as a religious holiday and as a general family event with the festive remnants of old pagan celebrations of spring, such as decorated eggs and chocolate bunnies. Like *Weihnachten*, Easter is celebrated over two days (*Ostersonntag und Ostermontag*) with the Monday being an official holiday. This is also true of Pentecost, known in German as *Pfingsten*. Though in the U.S. this holiday is only marked in churches, *Pfingstsonntag und Pfingstmontag* are legal holidays in all the German-speaking countries.

What do you believe in?

As in the United States, there exists a legal separation of church and state, so Germany has no official church and freedom of religion is guaranteed under the Basic Law. In contrast to the United States, however, churches do have the ability to levy taxes on their members, which are then withheld from their salaries and passed on then to the church's central organization. In order to avoid paying this tax, known as *Kirchensteuer,* one must go through a process of declaring oneself to be not a member of any church. About one-third of the German population has taken this course of action, and though many more do not attend church or identify themselves as belonging to a congregation, they do not go through the process of terminating their membership. Often, people cite their wish of wanting to leave open the possibility of having a church wedding as one reason for not severing church ties.

Two-thirds of the German population claim Christian belief, 26.3 million of whom profess the *evangelische Konfession* (Protestant) and 26.6 million the *römisch-katholische Konfession.* This division lies mostly along geographic lines; the north and east are predominantly Protestant, while the south and west are predominantly Catholic. Approximately 3.3 million practicing Muslims live in Germany, while the number of *Juden* (Jews), which stood at over 600,000 when the Nazis came to power in 1933 but plummeted to 15,000 by the end of the Second World War, has now risen again to about 200,000, due largely to emigration from former Soviet republics.

Switzerland also has a nearly equal proportion of Catholics and Protestants (41% vs. 40% of Swiss nationals). While the Swiss constitution recognizes no state religion and guarantees freedom of worship for all, cantons do have the right to proclaim official churches. In Austria, however, the overwhelming majority (over 74%) are Roman Catholic, with 2.2% of the population professing Orthodox Christianity, and over 4% Islam. There is some discrepancy, however, as to how many Jews now live in Austria. Government figures place the number at over 8000, 7000 of whom live in and around Vienna, but others calculate the number at closer to 15,000, still far below even 1% of the total population.

Islam has been recognized by the Austrian government since the early 20th century, when Bosnia was part of the Austro-Hungarian empire. Buddhism has also been recognized as a religion since 1983. Switzerland, however, does not recognize Buddhism, meaning that Buddhist congregations cannot claim tax-exempt status and enjoy other rights of protection of property that recognized religions do. The issue of recognition has been particularly debated in Germany as the Church of Scientology has fought for official status for years, though it has not been granted.

Self-Evaluation

When listening, I can understand (Hören)

– information given by telephone: *Guten Tag, Sie sind verbunden mit …*

– dates (days and months)

In written texts, I can understand (Lesen)

– invitations to special events: *Es ist so weit. Wir heiraten …*

– expressions of acceptance and regrets: *Ich komme gern. / Leider kann ich nicht kommen, denn …*

– simple diary-style descriptions of festivities: *Nikolaustag*

I can produce the following oral structures (Sprechen)

– stating the current date and my birthday: *Heute ist der 31. Dezember. / Ich habe am 10. Januar Geburtstag.*

– giving a cause or reason for something: *Ich mache gern Sport, denn ich will fit bleiben.*

– expression of good wishes and congratulations: *Alles Gute zum Geburtstag!*

I can produce the following written texts (Schreiben)

– accepting or declining invitations: *Lieber …, vielen Dank für die Einladung. Ich komme …*

– an invitation: *Liebe …, ich feiere meinen Geburtstag … Herzliche Grüße …*

– a postcard from vacation: *Lieber …, ich bin in Wien. Die Stadt gefällt mir sehr gut. Jeden Tag …*

– a short letter about my work and daily routine: *Liebe …, vielen Dank für Deinen Brief. Seit drei Monaten arbeite ich nun schon …*

– a short description of a holiday: *Hier feiern wir Silvester meistens mit Freunden oder mit der Familie.*

Review Stations/Exam Training

Wiederholungsstationen	Review Stations

Seite 147 — page 147

die Pluralendung, -en	*plural ending*
der Vokalwechsel, -	*vowel change*
die Wiederholungsstation, -en	*review station*

Seite 150 — page 150

die Lösung, -en	solution
der Zimmerschlüssel, -	room key

Seite 152 — page 152

der Unterschied, -e	difference

Seite 153 — page 153

die Deutsch-Prüfung, -en	*German examination*
die Konjunktion, -en	*conjunction*
das Kunstmuseum, -museen	*art museum*
der Unfall, ¨e	accident
Vietnam (nur Singular)	*Vietnam*
die Zugfahrt, -en	*train trip*

Seite 155 — page 155

hin·fahren; du fährst hin, er fährt hin, er ist hingefahren	to travel (to a destination)
Prüfungstraining	exam training

Seite 156 — page 156

das Fragewort, ¨er	*question word, interrogative*
lösen	to solve
die Mitteilung, -en	communication, message
prüfen	to test, examine
die Sekunde, -n	second
der Zettel, -	slip of paper, note

Seite 157 — page 157

die Zimmernummer, n	room number

Seite 158 — page 158

die Autowerkstatt, ¨en	*auto repair shop*
der Fahrer, -	driver
der Fahrgast, ¨e	*passenger*
der Fluggast, ¨e	*flight passenger*
das Gewitter, -	storm
der Grillplatz, ¨e	*barbeque spot*
die Lese-Zeit, -en	*time for reading*
die Privatperson, -en	*private individual*
der/die Reisende, -	*traveler*
schließen; er hat geschlossen	to close

sitzen bleiben; er ist sitzen geblieben	to remain seated
der U-Bahnhof, ¨e	*commuter train station*

Seite 159 — page 159

der Antwortbogen, ¨	*answer sheet*
deshalb	therefore
die Führerscheinprüfung, -en	*drivers license examination*
die Grillparty, -s	*barbeque party*
der Lesetext, -e	*reading text*
die Notiz, -en	note
trotzdem	in spite of that
übertragen; du überträgst, er überträgt, er hat übertragen	transfer, copy over

Seite 160 — page 160

bearbeiten	*to work on*
der Hobbyraum, ¨e	*hobby room, workshop*
der Keller, -	basement
das Möbelstück, -e	*piece of furniture*
restliche	remaining
usw.	*etc.*

Seite 161 — page 161

abends	evenings
der Altbau, -ten	*vintage building*
die Bezahlung, -en	*payment*
Deutsch für Ausländer	*German for foreigners*
das Ehepaar, -e	*married couple*
der Ferienjob, -s	*vacation job*
die Garantie, -n	guarantee
der Hersteller, -	*manufacturer*
das Herz, -en	heart
kompetent	*competent*
das Modem, -s	*modem*
die Musikschule, -n	*music school*
offen	open
der PC, -s	*PC*
der Sommerurlaub, -e	*summer vacation/holiday*
die Sprachferien (nur Plural)	*language vacation (vacation spent learning)*
die Sprachkenntnis, -se	*language skill*
verbessern	to improve
ziehen; er ist gezogen	to move (house)

Seite 162 — page 162

die Bibliothek, -en	library
das Blumengeschäft, -e	*flower shop*
das Mittagsmenü, -s	*lunch menu*
nähere	here: more, detailed
der Salatteller, -	*salad plate*
separat	*separate*
das Team, s	team (not usually athletic)
das Verständnis (nur Singular)	*understanding*

Seite 163   page 163

außerdem	besides
fehlend	*missing*
das Geschlecht, -er	*gender*
das Kreuz, -e	*here:* X
männlich	masculine
das Nachbarland, ̈er	*neighboring country*
das Studentenheim, -e	*residence hall, dormitory*
das Studienfach, ̈er	*field of study*
der Studienplatz, ̈e	*seat at university (being admitted)*
die Tortellini (nur Plural)	*tortellini*
weiblich	feminine

Seite 164   page 164

der Adressat, -en	*addresse*
formell	*formally*
informell	*informally*
der/die Prüfer/in, -/nen	*examiner*
sauber	cleanly

Seite 165   page 165

das Alphabet, -e	alphabet
der Ehepartner, -	*spouse*
die Handynummer, -n	cell phone number
mündlich	orally
der Stadtteil, -e	*neighborhood or district of a city*
der/die Teilnehmende, -en	the one participating
überlegen	to consider
die Vorstellung, -en	introduction

Seite 166   page 166

der Teilnehmer, -	participant
die Übersichtsseite, -n	*overview page*

Answers to the XXL Exercises

Chapter 8

7 **a** My brother was in Mexico in the summer. He is training as a hotel professional and did an internship in Cancun. He really learned a lot there. **b** Sonia, you're looking for a job, aren't you? Servitec Company (The company Servitec) needs people with good language skills. I found an ad on the internet.

8 **a** Für wie lange sind Sie in Deutschland? – Drei Monate. Und was studieren Sie? – Ich studiere Wirtschaft und Marketing. – Sie machen ein Praktikum bei Siemens, nicht? Wie lange studieren Sie schon? – Vier Wochen. **b** Was hast du/haben Sie am Wochenende gemacht? – Ich hatte Besuch. Ein Freund/Eine Freundin aus der Schweiz war hier und wir haben viel erzählt. Was hast Du/haben Sie gemacht? – Wir waren auf einer Hochzeit. Das war sehr schön. Wir haben bis fünf Uhr morgens getanzt.

Chapter 9

7 **a** You all have to visit the Hemingway House in Chicago sometime. Ernest Hemingway's family lived there. **b** Ms. Merten, why don't you give a call to the information desk? Maybe there are still tickets for the football game. **c** What does "continental breakfast" mean? Do you get orange juice with that, too?

8 **a** Entschuldigung, darf/kann ich Sie etwas fragen? Wo kann man Eintrittskarten für das Museum kaufen? – Es tut mir leid, das weiß ich nicht. Fragen Sie lieber bei der Touristeninformation./Am besten fragen Sie bei der Touristeninformation. **b** Komm, wir müssen um neun im Restaurant sein. – Mist! Ich habe meine Tasche vergessen. **c** Entschuldigung, können Sie mir helfen? – Ja, natürlich. – Wo muss man die Fahrkarten stempeln/entwerten?

Chapter 10

4 possible response: My friend's throat has been hurting for three days and she/he has a bad headache. His/her head is really hot, too. She/he coughs a lot and she/he didn't sleep the entire night. Now she/he has a stomache as well and she/he has no more appetite.

5 possible response: Der Arzt sagt, du musst ein paar Tage zu Hause im Bett bleiben und viel Wasser trinken. Er/sie gibt dir Tabletten und du sollst eine pro Tag nehmen. Du darfst nicht rauchen.

6 **a** Wo soll/muss ich unterschreiben? – Hier, bitte. **b** Sieh mal, mein Bein ist ganz dick! – Sollen wir zum Arzt gehen? **c** Hast du deinen Führerschein dabei? – Ich habe keinen Führerschein. **d** Wie geht es Edward? Hat er noch Rückenschmerzen? – Ja, immer noch, er kann keinen Sport machen.

Chapter 11

6 **a** Excuse me, how far is it to the cathedral? – That's not far at all, you can go there on foot. **b** Where is the Hotel Novotel? – It's right in the (city) center.

7 **a** Am Freitag fahre ich nach Hamm. Meine Eltern wohnen da/dort (Dort wohnen meine Eltern). **b** Ich gehe/fahre zu Karl. Wir wollen das Fußballspiel sehen. **c** Herr Monroe ist am Telefon/spricht gerade. – Es tut mir leid, ich habe jetzt keine Zeit. **d** Entschuldigung, gibt es/ist hier in der Nähe eine Bushaltestelle? – Ja, da drüben/da gegenüber.

Chapter 12

7 **a** How long have you all had the DVD player? – For two weeks. **b** Can you repair the computer by next week? – No problem, it will be done on Tuesday. **c** Would you please turn off the TV? I don't like to watch TV during dinner. – Too bad, the movie was interesting. **d** When can I call you tomorrow? – Tomorrow morning. I am in the office from 8 o'clock on.

8 **a** Könnten Sie das bitte nochmal erklären? – Ja, natürlich/klar. **b** Wo ist denn Andreas? – Beim Training. Am Freitag hat er ein Spiel. **c** Können wir eine Pause machen? – Ja, aber (zu)erst machen wir die Übung. **d** Mach/Macht/Machen Sie bitte die Fenster zu! – Aber sie sind (doch) schon zu!

Chapter 13

7 **a** How do you like the shoes (over) there? – Those are too expensive. **b** Which jacket should I put on? – This one here, it suits you/looks good on you. **c** Harald looks better with a shirt. – You think so? **d** Which color do you like best? – I like red best.

8 **a** Welchen Text sollen wir lesen? – Diesen hier. Er ist/steht auf Seite 66. **b** Die Bluse passt mir nicht. – Die Größe stimmt nicht. Welche Größe brauchen Sie? **c** Rex, gehört dir das Wörterbuch/ist das dein Wörterbuch? – Nein, das gehört mir nicht (es gehört dir). **d** Fahren wir mit dem Auto? – Ich gehe lieber zu Fuß.

Chapter 14

5 **a** My wife is now the director at her school. – Congratulations! **b** I met your boss yesterday. – What did you think of him? **c** I like studying with this book because it's fun. – Yeah, it's great! **d** Ms. Wesel, are you coming to our celebration/party too? – I don't know yet. – Please let me know by Monday.

6 **a** Welcher Tag ist heute? – Der dritte Oktober. **b** Ich möchte gern meinen Termin nach hinten verschieben. – Können Sie am dreiundzwanzigsten Mai kommen? Das ist ein Freitag. **c** Lena wird am Samstag 30, geht ihr auch zu ihrer Feier/Party? – Ja, sollen wir euch abholen? **d** Dani darf nicht fahren, denn er hat Wein getrunken. – OK, wir rufen ein Taxi. **e** Peter hat morgen eine Prüfung, aber er hat nichts gemacht. – Ich verstehe ihn nicht.

Answers to the Workbook Exercises

Lektion 8

A

1 Kaufmann/Kauffrau, Journalist/Journalistin, Hotelfachmann/ Hotelfachfrau, Verkäufer/Verkäuferin, Architekt/ Architektin, Lehrer/Lehrerin, Flugbegleiter/Flugbegleiterin, Hausmann/Hausfrau

3 **a** Job **b** Studierst ... – ... Ausbildung ... **c** Studieren ... – ... arbeite als ... **d** ... Journalist **e** ... zur Schule – ... Klasse

4 *Musterlösung*:
a Bist du Kauffrau? **b** Was bist du von Beruf? **c** Was studierst du? **d** Was ist sie von Beruf?

5 *Musterlösung*:
Mein Name ist Claudia Sassone. Ich komme aus Italien, aus Triest. Meine Hobbys sind Lesen und Tanzen. Ich spiele auch sehr gerne Fußball und Tischtennis. Deutsch habe ich in Italien gelernt. Zurzeit mache ich eine Ausbildung als Verlagskauffrau.

6 Lehrer • Programmierer • Verkäufer • Schüler • Partner

8 **a** Computer ... teuer – aber ... möchte ... Fernseher. **b** Leider ... Wiedersehen ... Donnerstag **c** ... Wörter verstehen ... **d** Meine Schwester ... Bruder ... keine Kinder

B

9 **a** Vor **b** Seit **c** Seit **d** Seit

10 **b** In Belgrad. **c** Vor zehn Jahren. **d** Seit einem Jahr. **e** Nein, ich arbeite als Programmierer.

11 **a** Vor **b** Seit **c** Vor **d** Seit **e** Vor

12 **a** vor einer Woche **b** vor drei Jahren **c** seit einem Monat
d seit einem Tag

13 ... einer Woche – ... acht Monaten – ... einem Jahr – ... sieben Wochen ... – ... einer Woche

14 **b** ... seit ... **c** ... am ... – Von ... bis ... **d** ... am ...
e ... seit ... – ... am ... vor ... **f** Am ... am ... – Um ... . vor ... **g** Im ...

16 **a** Wann haben Sie als Ärztin gearbeitet? – Seit wann arbeiten Sie als Ärztin? **b** Wie lange lernen Sie schon Deutsch? – Wann haben Sie den Deutschkurs in Berlin gemacht? **c** Seit wann fährst du jedes Jahr nach Italien? – Wann bist du nach Italien gefahren?

17 **b** Mein Mann arbeitet <u>seit</u> acht Monaten als Programmierer. **c** <u>Vor</u> drei Wochen haben wir eine schöne Wohnung gefunden. **d** Ich suche <u>seit</u> einem Jahr eine Arbeit als Hotelfachfrau **e** <u>Seit</u> einer Woche mache ich wieder einen Deutschkurs.

18 **a** Ich bin 1985 in Buenos Aires geboren. **b** Seit 2 Jahren studiere ich. **c** Vor 3 Monaten bin ich nach Deutschland gekommen. **d** Vor 2 Monaten habe ich einen Deutschkurs gemacht. **e** Seit einem Monat mache ich ein Praktikum.

C

19 Wo <u>wart</u> ihr denn am Samstag?
Ich <u>war</u> zu Hause.
Wir <u>waren</u> auch zu Hause, wir <u>hatten</u> Besuch. Meine Eltern <u>waren</u> da.
Ich <u>war</u> in der Schule. Meine Kinder <u>hatten</u> Schulfest. Und wo <u>warst</u> du? <u>Hattest</u> du ein schönes Wochenende?
Ich <u>war</u> zu Hause, ich <u>habe</u> Kuchen gemacht und ... Ich <u>hatte</u> doch Geburtstag, aber ihr <u>seid</u> nicht gekommen. Warum denn nicht?

		sein		haben
ich	bin	war	habe	hatte
du	bist	warst	hast	hattest
er/es/sie	ist	war	hat	hatte
wir	sind	waren	haben	hatten
ihr	seid	wart	habt	hattet
sie/Sie	sind	waren	haben	hatten

20 **a** ... hatte ... . sind ... . war ... war ... . hatten ... – ... ist ... – ... bin ... ! ... war ... . hatte ...
b ... ist ..., ... ist ..., ... ist ... . habe ... – ... wart ... – ... waren ... – ... war ... Hattet ... – ... war ... hatten ...

21 **a** ... war ... hatte ... – ... hatte ... war ... **b** ... waren ... hat ... habt ... – ... waren ... war ... haben ... **c** Warst ... – ... waren ...

22 Ich hatte noch keine Arbeit – ich war arbeitslos. Ich hatte auch keine Freunde. Mein Bruder war schon seit einem Jahr in Deutschland. Er hatte schon eine Arbeit. ... Ich habe einen Sprachkurs gemacht. Dann habe ich eine Arbeit gesucht. Dann habe ich auch Freunde gefunden.

D

23 **a** der Frühling: März, April, Mai **b** der Sommer: Juni, Juli, August **c** der Herbst: September, Oktober, November **d** der Winter: Dezember, Januar, Februar

24 Stefanie: Im März; Heiko: Im Mai; Julia: Im August; Annette: Im Oktober; Mirko: Im Dezember

25 **a** ... am ... – ... von ... bis ... **b** Im ... im ... **c** Im ... **d** ... für ... **e** Um ... **f** ... für ...

26 1 c 2 b 3 b

E

27 **a** 1 ... um 6 Uhr früh anfangen und bis 14 Uhr arbeiten. 2 ... ich bekomme nur 900 € pro Monat. 3 ... als Telefonistin in einem Call Center. 4 Die Arbeit ist auch sehr langweilig. 5 ... seit Mitte Juni ... 6 Im Oktober fängt ja meine Ausbildung als Hotelfachfrau an!!! 7 Das finde ich nicht gut.
b *Musterlösung*:
Seit zwei Monaten ... als Architektin in Hannover. ... arbeite von 9 Uhr 30 bis 18 Uhr 30. ... sehr nett und sympathisch. ... 30 Tage ...

Answers to the Workbook Exercises

Lektion 9

A

1 **b** Wir **c** Jens und Olga **d** Ich **e** Maria **f** Sie **g** Ihr
   ich/er/sie muss • du musst • wir/sie/Sie müssen •
   ihr müsst

2 **b** Wo **müssen** wir **warten**? **c** Was **muss** man hier
   machen? **d** Wir **müssen** noch das Wechselgeld
   nehmen. e Peter **muss** noch **bezahlen.**

3 **a** Sie muss noch das Zimmer aufräumen. **b** Du musst
   noch Hausaufgaben machen. **c** Ihr müsst morgen früh
   einen Test schreiben! **d** Du musst aufstehen!

4 **b** Können ... **c** Willst ... **d** ... kann ... **e** Möchtet ...
   f ... muss ... **g** ... will ...

5 **a** ... musst ... – ... will ... . muss ... **b** ... könnt ...
   müsst ... **c** ... musst ... . kann ... **d** ... kannst ... – ...
   will ...
   e ... müssen ... **f** ... kann ... muss ...

6 **a** ▲Och, nein! ◆ Doch, ich muss jetzt gehen.
   b ■ Kannst du heute kommen? ● Nein, tut mir Leid.
   ■ Du kannst kommen, da bin ich sicher, aber du willst
   nicht kommen. **c** ▼ Ich kann schon lesen. ● Das
   glaube ich nicht. ▼ Doch, ich kann schon lesen. **d** ■
   Wir wollen jetzt fernsehen. ◆ Nein, jetzt nicht! ■ Wir
   wollen aber fernsehen. ◆ Ihr könnt aber jetzt nicht!

B

8 Warten Sie einen Moment! ↘ Unterschreiben Sie hier!
   ↘ Bezahlen Sie an der Kasse? ↗ Kaufen Sie doch einen
   Stadtplan! ↘ Reservieren Sie die Tickets? ↗

9 Kommen Sie heute? – Kommen Sie heute um fünf! –
   Schlafen Sie gut! – Essen Sie ein Brötchen! – Essen Sie
   einen Apfel! – Trinken Sie viel Milch? – Kaufen Sie
   eine Fahrkarte? – Gehen Sie zur Touristeninformation!

10 Gehst du ... ? Geh ... ! Geht ihr ... ? Geht ... ! •
   Kommst du ...? Komm ... ! Kommt ihr ... ?
   Kommt ... ! • Rufst du ... ? Ruf ... ! Ruft ihr ... ?
   Ruft ... ! • Stehst du ... ? Steh ... ! Steht ihr ... ?
   Steht ... ! • Arbeitest du ... ? Arbeite ... ! Arbeitet ihr
   ... ? Arbeitet ... ! • Sprichst du ...? Sprich ... ! Sprecht
   ihr ... ? Sprecht ... ! • Liest du ... ? Lies ... ! Lest
   ihr ... ? Lest ... ! • Nimmst du ... ? Nimm ... ! Nehmt
   ihr ... ? Nehmt ... ! • Isst du ... ? Iss ... ! Esst ihr ... ?
   Esst ... ! • Schläfst du ... ? Schlaf ... ! Schlaft ihr ... ?
   Schlaft ... !

11 **a** ... oder gehen Sie ein bisschen spazieren! – Machen
   Sie einen Kurs! – Lesen Sie die Anzeigen in der
   Zeitung! Fragen Sie Ihre Lehrerin! **b** Rufen Sie die
   Touristeninformation an! – Gehen Sie an die
   Abendkasse!

12 **a** ... geh schwimmen! Besuch die Oma oder spiel
   Fußball oder ruf Freunde an! Aber sei um sechs Uhr
   zu Hause!
   b ... geht schwimmen! Besucht die Oma oder spielt
   Fußball oder ruft Freunde an! Aber seid um sechs Uhr
   zu Hause!

13 **a** ..., seid bitte leise! **b** ... bitte das Fenster zu! – ...,
   macht bitte das Fenster zu! **c** ..., warte bitte einen
   Moment! – ..., warten Sie bitte einen Moment! **d** ...,
   komm bitte um acht Uhr! – ..., kommen Sie bitte um
   acht Uhr! **e** ..., bezahl an der Kasse! – ..., bezahlen Sie
   an der Kasse! **f** ..., unterschreibt bitte hier! – ...,
   unterschreiben Sie bitte hier!
   g ..., sieh bitte im Wörterbuch nach! – ..., seht bitte
   im Wörterbuch nach!

14 **a** Arbeite doch nicht so viel! – Mach doch Urlaub!
   b Geh doch ins Museum! **c** Kommen Sie bitte um fünf
   Uhr! **d** Sprechen Sie bitte langsam! **e** Nimm mich
   bitte mit.

C

16 **a** ... dürfen ... **b** ... darfst ... **c** ... dürft ... **d** Darf ...
   e ... dürfen ... **f** Darf ...

17 **a** 1 Ich kann nicht mitfahren. 2 Ich darf nicht
   mitfahren. 3 Ich will nicht mitfahren. 4 Ich möchte
   gern mitfahren.
   b 1 Hier müssen wir warten. 2 Hier dürfen wir fahren.

D

19 **a** ... Eintritt ... **b** ... Ermäßigung **c** ...
   Sehenswürdigkeiten ... **d** ... besichtigen? ... Führung ...

20 **b** ... berühmt. ... gemütlich. **c** ... jung. ... wütend.
   d ... preiswert. ... teuer. **e** ... wenig. ... viel.

21 *Musterlösung*:
   ... eine Stadtrundfahrt gemacht. Danach sind wir ins
   Zentrum gefahren und haben den Stephansdom
   besichtigt. Gestern Abend waren wir im Schloss
   Schönbrunn. Am Samstag haben wir einen Ausflug an
   den Neusiedler See gemacht. ...

E

23 **a** Was heißt „Ziel auswählen"?/Was bedeutet „Ziel
   auswählen"? – ... Das Wort verstehe ich nicht. Was
   heißt „stempeln"?/Was bedeutet „stempeln"? Können
   Sie das bitte erklären?
   b Können Sie das bitte wiederholen? – Was heißt ... ?/
   Was bedeutet ...?

24 **b** wiederholen **c** auswählen **d** die Halbpension **e** das
   Konzert **f** der Haushalt **g** täglich **h** das Auto

25

15.7.	20.7.	
Tag der Ankunft	Tag der vorauss. Abreise	
Murray	Susan	12.05.1980
Name	Vorname	Geburtsdatum
10897 Berlin		irisch
Postleitzahl, Ort		Staatsangehörigkeit
Kantstraße 34	Deutschland	
Straße, Hausnummer	Staat	

Answers to the Workbook Exercises

Lektion 10

A

1 (links) (rechts)
Kopf   Auge
Hals   Nase
Finger   Mund
Hand   Ohr
Arm   Bauch
Rücken   Bein

2 fünf Finger – zwei Füße – zwei Augen – zwei Ohren – zwei Hände – zwei Arme – zwei Beine

3

der Kopf	**das** Ohr	**die** Nase	**die** Ohren
Fuß	Auge	Hand	Beine
Hals	Bein		Hände
Mund			Arme
Finger			Augen
Rücken			Zähne
Bauch			Finger
Arm			Füße

4 **a** ... Ihre ... – ... meine ... **b** ... dein ... – ... mein ... **c** ... meine ... – ... deine ... – ... meine ... **d** ... deine ... – ... meine ... **e** ... Ihr ... **f** Deine ... **g** ... Ihre ... **h** ... Ihre ...

B

5
Corinna
(Ihr) Familienname ...
(Ihr) Auge ...
(Ihr(e)) Wohnung ...
(Ihr(e)) Eltern ...

6 **b** ... ihre ... **c** ... ihre ... **d** ... ihr ... **e** ... sein ... **f** ... seine ... **g** ... seine ...

7 Ihre ... ihr ... . Ihr ... . Ihre ... ihr ... ihre ... . Ihre ... . Ihr ... . Seine ... .

8 *Musterlösung*:
Also, sein Name ist Ivano. Er kommt aus Italien. Seine ganze Familie lebt seit 25 Jahren in Deutschland. Seine Schwester und seine drei Brüder sind in Deutschland geboren. Seine Eltern haben ein Restaurant. Spaghetti schmecken dort sehr gut.

10 **a** Unsere ... **b** Unsere ... unsere ... **c** ... unser ... **d** ... ihre ... **e** ... euer ... **f** ... eure ...

11 **b** Ist das ein Fahrkartenautomat? **c** Lädst du den Tennislehrer auch ein? **d** Anja möchte den Papagei untersuchen. **e** Oje! Wie sieht denn der Fuß aus? Er ist ja ganz dick! **f** Er hat einen interessanten Job. **g** Der Job ist leider langweilig.

12 **b** ... sein ... **c** ... ihren ... **d** ... seinen ... **e** ... meinen ...

13 meine, deine
seine, ihre
unsere, eure   } Zeitschrift
ihre, Ihre

	Führerschein	Auto	Zeitschrift
Ich habe	meinen	mein	meine
Hast du	deinen	dein	deine
Er hat	seinen	sein	seine
Sie hat	ihren	ihr	ihre
Wir haben	unseren	unser	unsere
Habt Ihr	euren	euer	eure
Sie haben	Ihren	Ihr	Ihre
Haben Sie	Ihren	Ihr	Ihre

14 **a** ... meinen ... **b** ... Ihren ... Ihre ... Ihr ... – ... Ihren ...
c ... unseren ... **d** ... seine ... **e** ... mein ...

C

15 ... sollst ... – ... soll ... – Soll ... – Sollen ... – ... sollt ... – Sollen ... – ... sollen ...

16 **b** Steh bitte endlich auf! **c** Du sollst bitte langsam sprechen. **d** Seid bitte leise! **e** Sie sollen bitte hier unterschreiben. **f** Kreuzen Sie bitte „Ja" oder „Nein" an!
g Fragen Sie bitte Herrn Müller! **h** Ihr sollt hier bitte warten! **i** Macht bitte die Musik leise! **j** Du sollst dein Zimmer aufräumen! **k** Iss nicht so viel Schokolade!

17 **a** ... musst ... **b** ... sollst/darfst ... **c** ... soll ... **d** ... müssen ... **e** ... soll/darf ... **f** ... müssen ... **g** ... sollst ... **h** ... sollen ... muss ... **i** ... muss ...

18 *Musterlösung*:
... Ich soll sein Lieblingsessen kochen und ich soll auch einen Kuchen machen. Ich soll für ihn auch fünf Flaschen Multivitaminsaft kaufen! Der Arzt hat gesagt, er soll viel trinken. Dann soll ich seine Freundin Theresa anrufen und sie einladen. ...

D/E

19 **b** Sehr geehrte Damen und Herren,

ich habe Ihre Anzeige in der Augsburger Zeitung gelesen und ich habe folgende Fragen:
Wie viel kostet ein Doppelzimmer mit Halbpension? Wie teuer ist ein 4-Bett-Zimmer mit Halbpension. Haben Sie auch Kinderermäßigung? Sind Ende Februar zwei Zimmer frei?

Vielen Dank im Voraus!

Mit freundlichen Grüßen ...

20 **b** ... verschieben **c** ... einladen **d** ... absagen
21 1 c 2 b 3 c

Lektion 11

A

1 **a** Gehen Sie geradeaus und die zweite Straße links. **b** Tut mir leid, ich bin auch fremd hier. **c** Gehen Sie hier nach links und immer geradeaus.

3 *Musterlösung*:
a Ist hier eine Bäckerei in der Nähe? **b** Gibt es hier eine Post? **c** Wo ist hier der Bahnhof? **d** Entschuldigung, ich suche die Wilhelmstraße.

4 *Musterlösung*:
Gehen Sie zuerst geradeaus und dann die erste Straße links. Gehen Sie weiter geradeaus und dann die dritte Straße rechts. Nach ca. 200 m sehen Sie schon das Kino.

5 B das Auto C das Fahrrad D der Zug E das Taxi F die Straßenbahn G das Flugzeug H die U-Bahn

6 a ... mit dem Bus. b ... mit dem Taxi, mit dem Fahrrad, mit dem Auto. c ... mit der U-Bahn, mit der Straßenbahn.
d Mit dem Flugzeug.

7 a Michael: Ich nehme den Bus. Frank: Ich nehme die U-Bahn. Gerd: ... Vielleicht fährt jetzt kein Bus mehr und auch keine Straßenbahn. ... Peter: ... Ich nehme ein Taxi.
b Michael: mit dem Bus; Frank: mit der U-Bahn; Gerd: zu Fuß; Peter: mit dem Taxi

B

9 1 Kino 2 Post 3 Restaurant 4 Bahnhof 5 Bank 6 Bushaltestelle 7 Hotel 8 Supermarkt 9 Apotheke 10 Bäckerei

10 b 3 c 2 d 6 e 4 f 5

11 a auf b in c neben d an e an f unter g hinter h über

12

(links)	(rechts)
auf	zwischen
unter	neben/auf
in	hinter
	auf

13 Auf dem Tisch. – In der Tasche. – Hinter dem Fernseher. – Auf dem Sofa. – Neben dem Telefon. – Unter dem Sofa. – Zwischen den Wörterbüchern.

14 dem Tisch, Sofa ... – der Tasche, ... – den Büchern, ...

15 b ... im ... c Im ... d ... auf dem ... e ... in der ... f ... in der ... g An der ...

16 b Das Restaurant „Taverne" in der Bahnhofstraße ist sehr gut. c Sie müssen an der Ampel nach rechts gehen. d Ich habe Manuela im Deutschkurs kennen gelernt. e Olga wartet an der Bushaltestelle.

17 Im Kino? Am Bahnhof? Im Café Paradiso? An der Bushaltestelle? An der U-Bahn-Station? Am Parkplatz? In der Disko? Im Fitnessstudio?

18 *Musterlösung*:
B ... Sie ist in der Praxis. C Timo arbeitet. Er ist im Studio. D Timo und Anja joggen. Sie sind im Park. E Timo und Hanna warten. Sie sind im Bahnhof. F Timo kauft Joggingschuhe. Er ist im Sportgeschäft. G Timo und Anton tanzen Tango. Sie sind zu Hause.

C

19 a Ich war bei Paul. Wir waren im Schwimmbad und dann in der Stadt. b Ich fahre zu Denis. Wir gehen ins Schwimmbad und dann in die Stadt. c Zur Apotheke, ich brauche Aspirin. d Was hast du in der Apotheke gekauft? e Ich war im Deutschkurs und dann beim Arzt. f Zuerst gehe ich in den Deutschkurs und dann

zum Arzt. g Bist du heute morgen mit dem Fahrrad in die Schule gefahren? Ich war nicht in der Schule, ich bin krank. h Gehst du mit ins Kino? Ach, ich habe keine Lust, ich war erst gestern im Kino. i In Leipzig. j Nach Berlin. k ... Ich bin schon um zehn Uhr nach Hause gegangen. ... Ich war erst um zwei Uhr zu Hause.

	Wo?		Wohin?
im	Schwimmbad	ins	Schwimmbad
in der	Stadt	in die	Stadt
in der	Apotheke	zur	Apotheke
im	Deutschkurs	in den	Deutschkurs
beim	Arzt	zum	Arzt
in der	Schule	in die	Schule
im	Kino	ins	Kino
in	Leipzig	nach	Berlin
zu	Hause	nach	Hause

20 a ... beim ... b ... zum ... c ... nach ... – ... zu ... d ... nach ... – ... in ... e ... nach ... – ... nach ... – ... in ... – ... in ... f ... zu ... – ... im ... g ... in ... – ... in der ... – ... in ... h Im ... i Nach ... – ... in die ... j ... zur ... – ... zur ... k ... nach ...

21 a Fährt die U-Bahn zum Flughafen? b Im September fahren wir in die Schweiz. c Ich gehe noch schnell zur Post. d Im Urlaub fahren wir in die USA. e Warst du schon beim Arzt? f Heute Abend sind wir zu Hause. g Am Samstag fahre ich zu Oma Anna. h Waren Sie schon in der Bank? i Ich bin müde. Ich gehe jetzt nach Hause.

22 *Musterlösung*:
B zum Kiosk C zum Bahnhof D nach Dresden E zum Blumenladen F ins Krankenhaus

23 *Musterlösung*:
... zur Bank gegangen und habe Geld geholt. Dann bin ich zum Kiosk gegangen und habe ein Buch für meine Mutter gekauft. Danach bin ich mit der Straßenbahn zum Bahnhof gefahren und bin mit dem Zug nach Dresden gefahren. Am Nachmittag war ich dann in Dresden. Ich bin noch zum Blumenladen gegangen und habe Blumen gekauft. Dann bin ich ins Krankenhaus gefahren.

D

25 a umsteigen, aussteigen, einsteigen b die Ankunft, die Abfahrt, der Fahrplan, der Schalter, die Durchsage, die Fahrkarte

26 b Wann fliegt dein Flugzeug ab? c Gibt es eine Ermäßigung für Jugendliche? d Holst du mich am Flughafen ab? e Wo ist denn hier eine Bushaltestelle? f Ist der Zug pünktlich?

27 a richtig b falsch c richtig

28 **a** ... umsteigen ... – fährt ... ab. ... kommen ... an.
b Hin und zurück ... einfach? – ... Verspätung – Circa ... – ... Kiosk ...

29 **b** ... in ... **c** ... am ... **d** ... um ... **e** Am ... **f** Nach ... um ... nach ... **g** ... im ...

30 1 Entschuldigung, auf welchem Gleis fährt der Zug nach Ulm? 2 Fährt hier der Bus nach Moosbach ab? 3 Entschuldigung, wie viel Verspätung hat der Zug? – Dann bekomme ich den Anschluss in Frankfurt nicht mehr.

Lektion 12

A

1 **a** Am ... um ... – ... von ... bis ... . für ... **b** Seit ... – ... vor ...

2 **b** ... nach dem Sport. **c** Beim Frühstück. **d** ... nach der Arbeit. **e** ... beim Abendessen. **f** Vor dem Essen. **g** Vor der Arbeit. **h** ... nach den Hausaufgaben.

3

vor/nach	dem Sport	dem Mittag-essen	der Arbeit	den Haus-aufgaben
bei	beim Sport	beim Mittag-essen	bei der Arbeit	bei den Haus-aufgaben

4 *Musterlösung*:
... Vor dem Frühstück geht er joggen. Beim Frühstück liest er Zeitung. Nach dem Frühstück fährt er mit dem Fahrrad zur Arbeit. Um 12 Uhr macht er Mittagspause. Beim Mittagessen spricht er mit seinen Kollegen. Nach dem Mittagessen geht er 20 Minuten spazieren. Dann arbeitet er bis 17 Uhr. Nach der Arbeit fährt er sofort nach Hause und macht das Abendessen. Beim Abendessen sieht er fern. Nach dem Abendessen telefoniert er mit seiner Mutter.

6 **a** Nach dem Unterricht. **b** Vor einem Monat. **c** Seit einer Woche. **d** Ja, nach den Feiertagen. **e** Ja, seit einer Stunde. **f** Vor zwei Wochen.

7

der ...	das ...	die ...	die ... n
nach *dem* Unterricht	nach *dem* Essen	nach *der* Schule	nach *den* Prüfungen
vor *dem* Kurs	vor *dem* Frühstück	vor *der* Reise	vor *den* Prüfungen
vor *einem* Monat	vor *einem* Jahr	vor *einer* Stunde	vor zwei Wochen
vor *einem* Tag	seit *einem* Jahr	seit *einer* Woche	seit drei Tage**n**

8 **a** ... seit ... **b** Vor einem ... **c** ... vor einer ... **d** ... nach der ... **e** Seit ... **f** Bei der ... **g** ... vor dem ... – ... nach dem ... **h** ... beim ... . Beim ..., beim ..., beim ...

B

9 in einem Tag – in einer Woche – in zwei Monaten – in einer Stunde – in einem Jahr – in zwei Wochen – in einem Monat – in zwei Jahren

10 **a** Ab ... – Bis ... **b** Bis ... – ... bis ... – ... ab ... **c** ... in ... – Bis ... **d** ... bis ... – ... in ...

11 **a** Bis ... – in ... **b** Um ... – ... ab ... **c** ... am ... ... – ... ab ... ... bis ... **d** Ab ... bis ...

12 **a** In 20 Minuten. **b** Ab 15 Uhr. **c** Nach 15 Uhr. **d** Bis 18 Uhr. **e** Ab 7 Uhr. **f** Seit halb neun.

13 **a** Wann ... ? **b** Wie lange ... ? **c** Bis wann ... ? **d** Ab wann ... ? **e** Wann ... ? **f** Seit wann ... ? **g** Wie lange ... ?

14 **b** Seit Montag. – Drei Tage. **c** Noch vier Tage. – Bis Freitag. **d** Im August. – Vor zwei Tagen. **e** In zwei Wochen. – Am Sonntag. **f** Bis September. – Zwei Monate. **g** Fünf Monate. – Seit fünf Monaten. **h** Vor fünf Monaten. – 2003.

15 *Musterlösung:*
● Meine Kaffeemaschine funktioniert nicht mehr. Bis wann können Sie sie reparieren?
▲ Bis Freitag.
● Noch eine ganze Woche! Geht es nicht bis Dienstag?
▲ Nein. Aber vielleicht geht es bis Mittwoch-nachmittag?
● Und ab wann kann ich am Mittwoch meine Kaffeemaschine abholen?
▲ Ab 15 Uhr. Wir haben bis 18 Uhr geöffnet.

C

17 **a** Würden Sie bitte vorbeikommen? **b** Könntest du mich bitte bald anrufen? Würdest du mich bitte bald anrufen?
c Könnten Sie bitte später noch einmal anrufen? Würden Sie bitte später noch einmal anrufen?
d Könntest du bitte Briefmarken kaufen? Würdest du bitte Briefmarken kaufen? **e** Könntest du mir bitte Feuer geben? Würdest du mir bitte Feuer geben?
f Könnten Sie bitte den Flug nach Wien buchen? Würden Sie bitte den Flug nach Wien buchen?
g Könntest du bitte dein Handy ausmachen? Würdest du bitte dein Handy ausmachen? **h** Könntest du mir bitte den Weg erklären? Würdest du mir bitte den Weg erklären?

18 **b** zu **c** an **d** aus

19 Die Balkontür ist zu. – Das Licht ist aus. – Das Radio ist aus. – Die Fenster sind auf.

20 *machen:* eine Party – einen Plan – das Essen – einen Kuchen – einen Kurs
anmachen, ausmachen: das Radio – den Computer – das Licht – die Heizung – den Herd
aufmachen, zumachen: die Tür, ein Buch, die Augen, den Schrank, das Fenster, den Mund, die/eine Dose, die/eine Flasche, den Laden

21 Mach bitte den Fernseher aus! – Aber der Fernseher ist schon aus!
Mach bitte die Haustür zu! – Aber die Haustür ist schon zu!

Mach bitte überall das Lícht aus! – Aber das Lícht ist
überall aús!
Ist das Rádio vielleicht noch án? – Nein! Das Rádio ist
aúch aus.

D

23 <u>a</u> B <u>b</u> B <u>c</u> A <u>d</u> B

E

25 <u>b</u> reparieren <u>c</u> das Telefon <u>d</u> danken <u>e</u> der Drucker
<u>f</u> übernachten <u>g</u> schließen <u>h</u> informieren
26 **2** Rechnung **3** Gebrauchsanweisung **4** Optiker
5 Kreuzung **6** Karten **7** Nachricht **8** Briefmarke
27 *Musterlösung:*
ich: das **Li**cht, lei**ch**t, **si**ch, **si**cher, strei**ch**en …
du: der **Du**rst, die **Du**sche, die **Du**rchsage …
er: das Bi**er**, die Lehr**er**in, der Brud**er**, besond**er**s …
es: all**es**, interessant, **es**sen, l**es**en, …
sie: **sie**ben, **sie**zen, der **Sie**g, …
28 *Musterlösung:* das Radio reparieren, der Fernseher
funktioniert, Tee trinken, Kaffee kochen, im Bett
bleiben …

Lektion 13

A

1 eine – ein – einen – einen – Das – der – die – den
2 **1** Jacke   **6** Rock
   2 Pullover   **7** Hemd
   3 Schuhe   **8** Bluse
   4 Kleid   **9** Mantel
   5 Hose
3 <u>a</u> Die – Der <u>b</u> Das – Den <u>c</u> Den – Die <u>d</u> Die <u>e</u> Der
4 <u>a</u> … der … – Der … – Den … <u>b</u> … den … – Den … –
…
die … – Die … <u>c</u> …die … – … die … – … die … <u>d</u> …
den … – Den …   <u>e</u> … der … <u>f</u> … das … – … das
… – Das … <u>g</u> … die … – … die …
5 <u>a</u> … Den können wir nicht nehmen. <u>b</u> Nein, den finde
ich teuer. <u>c</u> Ja, finde ich auch. Der war gar nicht teuer.
<u>d</u> Das war klasse! <u>e</u> Das habe ich seit drei Monaten.
Mit dem fahren wir nach Spanien. <u>f</u> Nein, den kenne
ich nicht. <u>g</u> Nein, der ist nicht gut. Nimm doch den
Apfelsaft!
<u>h</u> Nimm doch den da!
6 <u>b</u> sehr schön ≠ hässlich <u>c</u> falsch ≠ richtig <u>d</u> langsam ≠
schnell <u>e</u> weiß ≠ schwarz <u>f</u> gesund ≠ krank <u>g</u> alt ≠ neu
<u>h</u> interessant ≠ langweilig <u>i</u> groß ≠ klein <u>j</u> schmal ≠
breit <u>k</u> kalt ≠ warm <u>l</u> laut ≠ leise
7 <u>a</u> Haus/Wohnung: … billig, günstig, alt, neu, modern,
schön, hässlich, groß, klein
<u>b</u> Straße: alt, neu, modern, schön, hässlich, breit,
schmal, groß, klein
<u>c</u> Buch: teuer, billig, günstig, alt, neu, schön, groß,
klein, gut, langweilig, interessant

<u>d</u> Text: alt, neu, schön, gut, langweilig, interessant
<u>e</u> Musik: alt, neu, modern, schön, hässlich, langsam,
schnell, laut, leise, gut, langweilig, interessant

B

9 <u>A</u> ■ Die passt *mir* super, aber die Farbe gefällt *mir*
nicht.
<u>B</u> ▲ Gefällt *dir* die Bluse nicht?
   ◆ Doch, die gefällt *mir* gut, aber sie ist sehr teuer.
<u>C</u> ■ Schau mal, die Hose gefällt *mir*.
   ▲ Aber die passt *dir* doch nicht.
<u>D</u> ◆ Entschuldigung, gehört die Zeitung *Ihnen*?
   ● Nein, die gehört *mir* nicht.
10 du/dir, Sie/Ihnen; er/ihm, sie/ihr; wir/uns;
ihr/euch, Sie/Ihnen; sie/ihnen
11 <u>b</u> Gehört das Fahrrad dir? <u>d</u> Gehört das Fahrrad ihr?
<u>e</u> Gehören die Bücher uns? <u>f</u> Gehören die Bücher
euch?
<u>g</u> Gehört das Haus ihnen? <u>h</u> Frau Koch, gehört das
Fahrrad Ihnen?
12 … und sie möchte ihm gefallen. …, es passt ihr aber
leider nicht. … Es gehört Mira, sie hat es ihr geliehen.
13 Ich bringe ihr ein Buch mit. – Ich bringe ihnen eine
CD mit. – Ich bringe euch ein Spiel mit.

C

16 <u>a</u> Ja, aber er spielt lieber Geige. <u>b</u> Beides zusammen.
<u>c</u> Beides zusammen: Fahrrad fahren und Geige spielen.
17 Frau Hagner geht gern ins Kino, aber ihr Mann geht
lieber tanzen.
Herr Klein sieht gern fern, aber seine Frau liest lieber.
Jamila spielt gern Fußball, aber ihr Bruder Omar sieht
lieber fern.
18 <u>a</u> … am besten. <u>b</u> … lieber … <u>c</u> … besser. <u>d</u> … mehr
… –
… am meisten … <u>e</u> … besser … <u>f</u> … mehr … <u>g</u> … am
liebsten …

D

19 <u>b</u> Welcher … – Dieser … <u>c</u> Welcher … – Dieser …
<u>d</u> Welches … – Dieses … <u>e</u> Welche … – Diese …
<u>f</u> Welcher … – Dieser …; Welches … – Dieses …;
Welche … – Diese …; Welcher … – Dieser …; Welche
… – Diese …
20 Welches Buch … – Dieses …; Welche Schuhe … –
Diese …; Welchen Fotoapparat … – Diesen …;
Welcher Koffer … – Dieser …; Welche Pizza … – Diese
…; Welchen Kuchen … – Diesen …; Welche
Brieftasche … – Diese …
21 <u>a</u> … dieses … – Welchen … <u>b</u> … welche … – Diese …
<u>c</u> Welches … – Dieses … <u>d</u> … dieses … – Welches … –
… dieses … <u>e</u> Welches … <u>f</u> Welcher … – Dieser …

E

23 <u>a</u> Sehr gut. <u>b</u> Ja, sie ist genau richtig. <u>c</u> Ja, aber sie
passt mir nicht. <u>d</u> Der blaue da. <u>e</u> Ich auch. <u>f</u> Hier
bitte.

24 <u>a</u> Im Obergeschoss. <u>b</u> Rot steht Ihnen sehr gut. <u>c</u> Tut mir Leid, den habe ich nur in Blau. <u>d</u> An der Kasse dort hinten rechts. <u>e</u> Nein, leider nur noch in dieser Größe. <u>f</u> Ja, gern. Was suchen Sie?

Lektion 14

A

1 <u>b</u> Der zwanzigste vierte. – Der zwanzigste April. <u>c</u> Der fünfzehnte sechste. – Der fünfzehnte Juni. <u>d</u> Der dreiundzwanzigste zweite. – Der dreiundzwanzigste Februar. <u>e</u> Der dritte zwölfte. – Der dritte Dezember. <u>f</u> Der erste erste. – Der erste Januar.

2 Stefanie: Am fünfzehnten März. Heiko: Am zweiten Mai. Maja: Am achtundzwanzigsten Juli. Sonja: Am siebzehnten September.
Bäckerei Kunz: Vom ersten (achten) bis (zum) fünfundzwanzigsten August
Herr Meinert: Vom dritten bis (zum) zwanzigsten Juli
Frau Braun: Vom achten bis (zum) neunzehnten November

3 <u>a</u> der 13.5. <u>b</u> für den 16. <u>c</u> am 24.3. <u>d</u> am 3.2.1980 <u>e</u> am 20.7. <u>f</u> am 5.4. um 10.30 Uhr

4 <u>a</u> ... später ... circa ... <u>b</u> ... bald ... <u>c</u> ... täglich ... <u>d</u> ... früh ... später ...

B

5 <u>a</u> Anja hat Timo zum Abendessen eingeladen. Sie findet ihn sehr sympathisch. Timo bringt Anton und Corinna mit. Sie sind auch Freunde von Anja.
<u>b</u> Timo hat seine Eltern nach Deutschland eingeladen. Natürlich besuchen sie ihn. Anja will sie auch kennen lernen.

6 ...
die Zeit bestimmt dich
die Zeit bestimmt ihn
die Zeit bestimmt uns
die Zeit bestimmt euch
die Zeit bestimmt sie

7 ... ...
du siehst die Sonne die Sonne sieht dich
er sieht die Sonne die Sonne sieht ihn
wir sehen die Sonne die Sonne sieht uns
ihr seht die Sonne die Sonne sieht euch
sie sehen die Sonne die Sonne sieht sie

8 <u>a</u> euch <u>b</u> dich <u>c</u> ... mich ... <u>d</u> ... sie ... – ... sie ... <u>e</u> ... es ... <u>f</u> ...ihn ... – ... dich ... <u>g</u> ... Sie ... <u>h</u> ... mich ...

9 <u>b</u> Ja, natürlich. Ich kenne ihn schon lange. <u>c</u> Ich finde sie sehr sympathisch. <u>d</u> Er arbeitet beim Fernsehen.

C

10 <u>a</u> ..., denn er hat nicht genug Geld. <u>b</u> ..., denn es ist schon so spät. <u>c</u> ..., denn heute Abend kommt Besuch. <u>d</u> ..., denn er muss noch Hausaufgaben machen.

11 *Musterlösung*:
<u>a</u> ..., denn sie macht gern Sport. <u>b</u> ..., denn er geht nicht gern zu Fuß. <u>c</u> ..., denn die Lehrerin will einen Test schreiben. <u>d</u> ..., denn sie will dort ihren Freund treffen.

12 <u>a</u> Anton und Timo gratulieren Corinna, denn sie hat heute Geburtstag. – Am Abend machen sie ein großes Fest, denn Corinna liebt Partys. <u>b</u> Ich komme gern, aber ich kann erst sehr spät kommen. – Ich mache einen Salat und ich bringe auch einen Kuchen mit. <u>c</u> Ich lerne Italienisch, denn ich finde die Sprache sehr schön. <u>d</u> Gehen wir tanzen oder bleiben wir zu Hause?

D/E

14 <u>b</u> Geburtstag feiern, Geburtstag haben <u>c</u> eine SMS schreiben, eine SMS schicken <u>d</u> zur Hochzeit gratulieren, zur Hochzeit einladen <u>e</u> ein Geschenk kaufen, ein Geschenk machen <u>f</u> eine Einladung verschicken, eine Einladung bekommen

16 <u>a</u> richtig <u>b</u> richtig <u>c</u> falsch

Wiederholungsstationen

2 *Musterlösung*:
-e: der Brief – die Briefe, der Tisch – die Tische, der Film – die Filme ...
ˉe: die Stadt – die Städte, der Sohn – die Söhne, der Gast – die Gäste ...
-er: das Kind – die Kinder, das Bild – die Bilder, das Schild – die Schilder, ...
ˉer: das Fahrrad – die Fahrräder, der Mann – die Männer, das Haus – die Häuser, ...
-n: der Name – die Namen, die Schule – die Schulen, die Straße – die Straßen, ...
-en: die Zahl – die Zahlen, die Uhr – die Uhren, die Sendung – die Sendungen, ...
–: das Zimmer – die Zimmer, der Koffer – die Koffer, der Arbeiter – die Arbeiter, ...
ˉ: der Bruder – die Brüder, der Apfel – die Äpfel, die Mutter – die Mütter, ...
-s: das Foto – die Fotos, das Auto – die Autos, das Büro – die Büros, ...

3 <u>a</u> Hilfst ... – ... hilft ... <u>b</u> Fährst ... <u>c</u> ... trifft ... <u>d</u> Gibt ... <u>e</u> ... spricht ... <u>f</u> ... nimmt ... <u>g</u> Isst ... <u>h</u> Liest ... <u>i</u> Gibst ... <u>j</u> Nimmst ... <u>k</u> ... siehst ... aus

4 der (Mantel); den (Arzt); den (Termin); der (Parkplatz); der (Ausgang); einen (Pullover); ein (Schokoladenkuchen); einen (Obstkuchen); ein (Fahrkartenautomat); einen (Bruder); ein (Brief)

5 <u>b</u> Ich habe keinen Hunger. <u>c</u> Haben Sie kein Telefon? <u>d</u> Ich liebe ihn nicht. <u>e</u> Ich fahre nicht mit dem Bus. <u>f</u> Sie hat keine Zeit. <u>g</u> Ich arbeite nicht als Verkäuferin. <u>h</u> Die Musik gefällt mir nicht.

7 <u>b</u> ... der ... <u>c</u> ... einen ... – ... der ... <u>d</u> ... einen ... – ... einen ... einen ... <u>e</u> ... einen ... – ... eine ... die ...

8 <u>a</u> Stunden <u>b</u> Stunden <u>c</u> Uhr <u>d</u> Stunden <u>e</u> Uhr

Answers to the Workbook Exercises

9 **b** Der zwölfte erste. **c** Der dritte sechste. **e** Am zweiundzwanzigsten siebten. **f** Am einunddreißigsten achten.

11 **a** Von … bis … von … bis …, am … am … bis … **b** Vor … **c** Am … **d** … im … **e** Am … um … **f** Seit … **g** Vor … **h** Im …

12 **a** … nach … **b** In … **c** … beim … **d** … bis … **e** … für … **f** … ab … **g** … in …

13 **b** Mein Zug kommt um 18 Uhr an. **c** Holst du mich in Frankfurt ab? **d** Der Bus fährt in zwei Minuten ab. **e** Sie sehen wirklich sehr gut aus. **f** Wir steigen in Wien um.
g Jörg, machst du bitte den Fernseher aus! **h** Ich rufe dich am Wochenende an. **i** Alex, bitte steh endlich auf und räum dein Zimmer auf!

14 **b** Möchtet … **c** … sollen … **d** Darf … **e** Können … **f** … kann … **g** Willst …

15 **b** Kannst … **c** Möchtest … **d** Sollen/Wollen … **e** … möchte/will … **f** … kann … **g** … müssen … **h** … wollt … **i** … dürfen …

16 **b** … seid … **c** … hat … **d** … bist … **e** Haben … **f** Hast … **g** … ist … **h** … haben … **i** Habt …

17 Ich habe gemacht. – Du hast gesucht. – Du hast geschrieben. – Er ist gegangen. – Sie haben gesagt. – Wir sind gekommen. – Wir haben gekauft. – Ihr habt geschlafen. – Ihr habt geantwortet. – Sie haben gespielt. – Sie sind gefahren. – Ihr habt gesprochen. – Sie sind gereist. – Ich habe gelernt. – Wir haben gegessen. – Ihr habt getrunken. – Du hast genommen.

18 **b** Fahr bitte Auto! – Ich bin Auto gefahren. – Fahrt bitte Auto! – Wir sind Auto gefahren.
c Lern bitte die Wörter! – Ich habe die Wörter gelernt. – Lernt bitte die Wörter! – Wir haben die Wörter gelernt.
d Iss bitte nicht so viel! – Ich habe nicht so viel gegessen. – Esst bitte nicht so viel! – Wir haben nicht so viel gegessen.
e Seien Sie bitte leise! – Wir sind leise gewesen./ Wir waren leise.
f Fragen Sie bitte die Lehrerin! – Wir haben die Lehrerin gefragt.

20 **a** … warst … **b** … war … **c** … war … warst … **d** … war … **e** … waren … hatten … **f** … hatte … **g** … war … **h** … war … **i** … wart … **j** … waren … **k** … hatten … waren …

21 *Musterlösung*:
Links ist ein Flugzeug, rechts sind es zwei. Links ist ein Hotel hinter der Post, rechts ein Restaurant. Links ist eine Apotheke neben der Post, aber rechts eine Bäckerei. Links ist ein Bus an der Haltestelle, rechts stehen Fahrräder. Vor dem Krankenhaus links steht ein Auto, vor dem Krankenhaus rechts steht ein Bus. Rechts gibt es keine U-Bahn. Links ist ein LKW auf dem Parkplatz, auf dem Parkplatz rechts ist nichts.

22 **a** Wer … ? **b** Wie … ? **c** Wen … ? **d** Woher … ? **e** Was … ? **f** Wo … ? **g** Was … ? **h** Wann … ? **i** Wohin … ? **j** Wie viel … ?

23 **a** …, denn … **b** … und … **c** … oder … **d** …, denn … . Aber …

24 **a** … beim … – … zum … **b** Aus … – In … **c** … zur … – … zur … **d** … zu … – … nach … **e** In der … – … in die … **f** … in der …

25 **a** Marco, könntest du bitte das Radio ausmachen?/ Würdest du bitte das Radio ausmachen? **b** Könnten Sie bitte langsam sprechen?/Würden Sie bitte langsam sprechen? **c** Könnten Sie das bitte noch einmal erklären?/Würden Sie das bitte noch einmal erklären? **d** Nina, könntest du bitte das Frühstück machen?/ Würdest du bitte das Frühstück machen?

26 **a** … am meisten. **b** … lieber … **c** … lieber. **d** … besser … am besten … **e** … am liebsten … am besten? – Am liebsten … am besten …

27 du: dir – Frau Hagner: Ihnen – Jonas: Ihm – Elke: ihr – wir: uns
Musterlösung:
Es gefällt mir. Gefällt es dir? Und gefällt es Ihnen, Frau Hagner? Ihm gefällt es sicher. Und ihr gefällt es auch. Natürlich gefällt es uns allen.

28 **a** … mich … ihn … – … dich … **b** … sie … – … sie … **c** … es … **d** … ihn … **e** … mich … mich … – … dich … dich … **f** … sie … – … sie …

29 **a** … ihren … – … ihr … – … ihren … **b** … mein … – … dein … dein … **c** … Ihre … **d** … deine … – Mein … meine … **e** … Ihr … – Seine … **f** … deinen … deinen … **g** … eure … – … unsere … **h** … Ihren … **i** … ihre …

vierundneunzig**94**   ANSWERS TO THE WORKBOOK EXERCISES

Answers to the Workbook Exercises

Start Deutsch 1 Die Prüfung

Hören

1	2	3	4	5	6	7	8	9	10	11	12	13	14	15
b	a	a	b	b	c	richtig	falsch	falsch	falsch	b	b	b	a	c

Lesen

1	2	3	4	5	6	7	8	9	10	11	12	13	14	15
falsch	richtig	richtig	falsch	richtig	b	b	a	b	b	richtig	falsch	falsch	falsch	falsch

Schreiben 1

1	2	3	4	5
Federico	Italien	männlich	Einzelzimmer	Architektur

Schreiben 2

Musterlösung:

Lieber ...

im Moment mache ich eine Reise, denn wir haben keinen Deutschkurs. Jetzt bin ich in Salzburg. Hier ist es sehr schön! Das Wetter ist schön, es regnet nur manchmal. Ich habe schon so viel gesehen! Heute möchte ich das Hundertwasserhaus besichtigen.

Herzliche Grüße

...

Answers to the Workbook Exercises

Test zu Lektion 8

1 **a** Ärztin **b** als Flugbegleiterin **c** Studentin – als **d** Hotel-fachmann
2 **a** Wann … **b** … wie lange / seit wann … **c** Seit wann …
   d Wann **e** Wann … **f** Seit wann …
3 … Ich habe viele Praktikumsbörsen gefunden und gleich mal ein paar Anzeigen gelesen. Dann habe ich die interessanten Angebote auf einen Zettel geschrieben. Das Angebot für ein Praktikum als Kindergärtnerin war besonders interessant. Ich habe sofort eine E-Mail geschrieben. Schon zehn Minuten später hatte ich eine Antwort von der Chefin. Sie war sehr freundlich. Ich habe die Stelle bekommen. Juchu! Ich war sehr glücklich und habe im Zimmer getanzt. Ein toller Tag!
4 **b** richtig **c** falsch **d** richtig **e** falsch **f** richtig **g** richtig **h** richtig

Test zu Lektion 9

1 *Musterlösung:* lesen; unterschreiben; abgeben …
2 **a** Seid … **b** Esst … **c** Gebt … **d** Zeig … **e** Lies … **f** Gib … ab
3 *Musterlösung:* … Dann muss ich zur Arbeit gehen. Jeden Tag muss ich acht Stunden arbeiten. Dann muss ich noch einkaufen. Zu Hause muss ich für meine Familie das Abendessen machen. Jeden Abend muss ich spätestens um 23 Uhr im Bett sein.
4 wollen – muss – müssen – Können – Möchten – darf – muss – Können – Können – müssen – Kann – dürfen

Test zu Lektion 10

1 **a** Ihre … **b** Deine … **c** … mein … **d** Dein … **e** Ihre … **f** Mein … **g** Ihr … **h** … eure ..
2 **a** Sein Hals … **b** Sein Fuß … **c** Ihre Ohren … **d** Ihr Bein …
3 **a** … soll viel trinken. **b** … soll eine Diät machen. **c** … soll mehr Obst essen.
4 2 Guten Morgen. Hier ist Bremer. Ich habe Zahnschmerzen. Wann kann ich vorbeikommen?
   3 Hm, diese Woche haben wir keinen Termin mehr frei. Aber Sie können nächsten Montag um 8 Uhr kommen.
   4 Das ist zu spät. Ich habe starke Schmerzen. Kann ich bitte heute noch kommen?
   5 Heute geht es nicht mehr. Der Herr Doktor ist nur noch eine halbe Stunde in der Praxis.
   6 Kann ich dann vielleicht morgen kommen?
   7 Mal sehen! – Ja, morgen von 16 bis 18 Uhr ist offene Sprechstunde. Da können Sie gern kommen.
   8 Gut, dann komme ich morgen Nachmittag um 16 Uhr vorbei! Danke. Auf Wiederhören!
   9 Bitte. Auf Wiederhören!

Test zu Lektion 11

1 **a** der **b** dem **c** dem **d** dem **e** dem
2 geradeaus – zum – Am – links – geradeaus – Am – rechts – in – geradeaus – erste – links
3 **b** D **c** C **d** A **e** F **f** E **g** B
4 *Musterlösung:* **a** Um 13.46 Uhr. **b** Mit der Straßenbahn Nummer 27. **c** … in Hannover. **d** … er hat Verspätung. **e** Gleich da drüben. **f** 6,5 Stunden. **g** Hin und zurück 84,60 Euro.

Test zu Lektion 12

1 **a** bei der **b** Vor dem **c** nach der **d** nach dem **e** Vor der **f** nach dem **g** beim **h** beim
2 **a** Könnten Sie bitte das Fenster zumachen?
   b Könnten Sie ihn bitte reparieren?
   c Würdest du bitte das Licht anmachen?
   d Könntest du das Radio bitte leise drehen?
   e Würdest du sie bitte ausmachen?
   f Könnten Sie später noch einmal anrufen?
3 **a** Bis … **b** In … **c** … ab … **d** Bis … am … bis … **e** In … **f** Ab … **g** In … **h** … bis …

Test zu Lektion 13

1 links   rechts
   die Jacke   die Bluse
   der Pullover   das Kleid
                  der Schuh
2 **a** die Gürtel **b** die T-Shirts **c** die Hemden **d** die Hosen **e** die Mäntel
3 **a** Das **b** Den **c** Das **d** Den – der **e** der **f** Das
4 **a** dir **b** mir – mir **c** dir **d** euch **e** Uns **f** Ihnen
5 **a** lieber – am liebsten **b** besser **c** besser **d** mehr **e** am meisten

Test zu Lektion 14

1 **a** siebzehnte vierte **b** dreiundzwanzigste fünfte **c** dreißigste dritte **d** erste zwölfte **e** siebenund-zwanzigste neunte **f** neunundzwanzigste elfte
2 **a** Der **b** Am **c** Vom … bis (zum) **d** Am **e** der
3 **a** es **b** ihn **c** mich – dich **d** sie **e** Sie **f** euch **g** sie
4 **a** Sebastian darf nicht Tennis spielen, denn der Arzt hat es verboten. **b** Maryam lernt Deutsch, denn sie möchte in Deutschland eine Arbeit finden. **c** Robert macht viel Sport, denn er will fit bleiben. **d** Selma geht am Samstagabend in die Disko, denn sie tanzt gerne. **e** Karin muss zum Zahnarzt, denn sie hat schon seit drei Tagen Zahnschmerzen. **f** Elke hat gestern viel eingekauft, denn sie macht heute eine Party.
5 *Musterlösung:* **a** Herzlichen Glückwunsch! **b** Frohe Weihnachten.
   c Viel Glück! **d** Frohe Ostern! **e** Alles Gute für euch.